Roz Morris runs her own business, TV News London Limited, a media training company, and television and radio news agency which supplies news to broadcasters in Britain and abroad. She worked as a freelance journalist and broadcaster for more than fifteen years for national newspapers, television and radio and had a careers advice column in *Options* magazine. She is chair of the London branch of Network, the organisation for senior professional women, and a member of the Women's National Commission, which represents women's organisations and their views to the Government.

Working for Yourself

How to Succeed at Being Your Own Boss

ROZ MORRIS

Phuong & Nhu 03/09/09

PIATKUS

Copyright © 1995 by Roz Morris
First published in the UK in 1995 by
Judy Piatkus (Publishers) Ltd
5 Windmill Street, London W1P 1HF

The moral rights of the author have been asserted

*A catalogue record for this book is available
from the British Library*

ISBN 0 7499 1335 5

Edited by Linda Zeff and Carol Franklin
Designed by Chris Warner
Typeset by Datix International Limited, Bungay, Suffolk
Printed and bound in Great Britain by
Biddles Ltd, Guildford & King's Lynn

Contents

Introduction

THERE ARE plenty of books about job-hunting, telling you how to apply for jobs, and how to brush yourself down and spruce yourself up for interviews. This is not one of them.

This book is about creating your own job for yourself and may be jobs for other people too. It's about how you can make the most of your existing talents, how you can use and expand them, and how you can learn new skills – including those of working for yourself and developing your own career.

These are the talents and skills you need today and tomorrow – because the days of full-time jobs being provided for almost everyone, whether by private organisations or by the State, are gone for ever. The concept of 'jobs for life' now has no reality, even for those fortunate enough to be still in work.

Ask people in what used to be considered 'safe' jobs – bank clerks, civil servants, coal miners, nurses, dockworkers, printers, telephone switchboard operators, soldiers, steelworkers, teachers, to name just a few: where are their jobs for life now?

Work is a changing animal; markets rise and fall, and technologies dictate staffing and output. This has been the case since the wheel was invented. Just as in the Industrial Revolution, mechanical improvements to weaving looms meant that fewer workers were able to produce more cloth, so computer technology has now reduced, and is continually cutting, the numbers of people needed in offices and factories.

It's not just the recession in trade which has caused staff reductions – known as 'downsizing' – in all kinds of businesses. Microchips are constantly speeding up processes and groups of workers with mechanical equipment are, more often than not, being replaced by single workers with computerised machines.

At the same time, larger organisations are finding it more cost efficient to reduce their staffing levels and, instead, to buy in many services from small companies. This downsizing is often a painful process for the staff concerned. But there *is* a brighter side to these changes.

Two hundred years ago the new machinery meant a mass move from working at home to working in factories. Now the new technology is reversing that trend.

WORKING FOR YOURSELF – THE WAY FORWARD

More than 3,000,000 people in Britain are now self-employed, many of them working from home. Over the past ten years, this represents a 30 per cent increase for men and a 40 per cent increase for women. More than two-fifths of all employment in the UK is now provided by businesses with fewer than 20 employees and those businesses create one-fifth of the country's gross domestic product. And there's more change to come. It's estimated that more than 5,000,000 people in Britain – one fifth of the working population – will be working from home by the year 2000.

Already, small and medium-sized businesses – that is, those which employ up to 500 people – provide just over 70 per cent of jobs in the European Union. For, while large organisations have been cutting back on staff, small businesses have, despite the recession, been the main creators of new jobs in Europe over the past decade. The same applies in North America.

This is today's jobs revolution and it's happening right now. But it's a revolution which, unlike comparable historic changes in work patterns, puts power into the hands of the small operators as well as big business. That's because powerful computer technology is not only available to big organisations, but also to people working on their own.

The easy availability of word processors, telephones, answerphones, modems and fax machines means it's now easier than ever before for people to work for themselves.

LEARNING FROM EXPERIENCE – A VALUABLE LESSON

As a freelance journalist and broadcaster, working for myself for nearly 20 years, I can see clearly how much things have changed – and changed for the better: how the small business, self-employed and freelance lifestyles have become more common and accepted as part of the normal working scene, and how much easier in practical terms it is now to work for yourself.

At the same time, I have seen how more and more of us who were brought up to think that someone else would always give us a full-time job have had to retrain ourselves to create our own work.

This book draws on my experience, and on the experience of a wide range of people who are already on the self-employed or freelance path; they all have different tales to tell. Because to be self-employed doesn't just mean taking on new responsibilities and learning new skills of administration and self-organisation, it also means taking on a different mindset from an employee.

When you are employed by someone else, you can afford to have the attitude that someone else should provide you with work. When you're working for yourself, you know that you have to go out and get the work yourself – not just today, but tomorrow and next week, and next year as well.

Jobs for life are now in the dustbin of history – and history has a very big dustbin. But you don't have to live in a dustbin, do you? So, whether you choose to be self-employed or whether you are forced by circumstances to go it alone, you have history on your side.

There is a jobs revolution going on right now and it means the old attitude that work is something employers give to you is no longer valid. Work is something *you* create. *You* are your business. The future is up to you.

1

The Jobs Revolution – Where Do You Fit In?

Change or the prospect of change will frighten everybody.

Sir John Harvey-Jones, former chairman of ICI and business author

SHOULD YOU WORK FOR YOURSELF?

WHEN IT'S SUCCESSFUL, you can't beat working for yourself – but it's not a lifestyle for everyone. This chapter is aimed at helping you find out whether working for yourself is the kind of life you can cope with, both mentally and physically.

The most important qualities you'll need to work for yourself are the willingness to accept the personal responsibility that goes with self-employment and the mental ability or mindset to cope with this extra burden of 'the buck stops here' accountability.

If your mindset is right, you'll appreciate that working for yourself is no riskier than life itself. In today's climate, you could be running the greatest risk by expecting someone else to employ you for life and make all your important decisions for you. You could be wrong. They could be wrong. You could end up together, outside in the rain, in the same queue for state benefits. The choice is yours.

So, should you consider working for yourself? Here are ten initial questions to ask yourself.

1. Do you *want* to work for yourself?
2. Do you want to turn a gap in the market into your own business?
3. Do you want to work from home?
4. Do you have to work for yourself because you've been made redundant?
5. Do you have to work for yourself because you're currently unemployed and see no other chance of obtaining an income above state benefits?
6. Do you want to turn a new invention into your own business?
7. Do you want to turn a new service into your own business?
8. Do you want work that will fit in with the demands of your children or dependent relatives?
9. Do you want to work part-time?
10. Do you want to turn a hobby into your own business?

If you can answer 'Yes' to any of these questions, this book is for you.

Weighing up the pros and cons

Before you make any decision about working for yourself, you need to consider what taking this step will mean.

20 advantages of working for yourself

1. You can control the work you do.
2. You can control your own career.
3. Your career prospects may improve.
4. You can work part-time, or only during school hours, if you wish.
5. You can organise your own hours.
6. You don't need to stick in a dead-end job.
7. You may gain in status.
8. You will have the prestige of running your own business.

9. You can benefit from new career prospects and have the freedom to try new markets.
10. You'll be free to test your own ideas.
11. You can pay less tax.
12. You may earn much more than you did when you were an employee.
13. You can claim equipment against tax.
14. You can claim car/van/some transport costs against tax.
15. If registered for VAT, you can reclaim it.
16. You can select, organise and pay for your own training.
17. You can choose your own staff or not to have any.
18. You'll have less stress because you won't have to deal with office politics.
19. Your quality of life will improve.
20. You can achieve increased job satisfaction.

20 disadvantages of working for yourself

1. You may get less pay, especially when you start.
2. You'll have no control over sources of your own work.
3. Your career prospects may diminish.
4. You may suffer a loss of status.
5. You'll have no job security.
6. You'll be responsible for income tax, National Insurance and VAT payments.
7. You'll be responsible for losses as well as profits.
8. You'll have no paid holidays.
9. You won't get sick pay – unless you pay for private health insurance.
10. You'll be responsible for insurance and equipment.
11. You'll be responsible for pensions.
12. You'll be responsible for health and safety in your office or work space.
13. You'll be responsible for paying off loans.
14. You may have to take out a second mortgage on your home.
15. You'll be responsible for keeping your own accounts.
16. You'll be responsible for phone bills, stationery, all equipment, etc.
17. You may always be on call, both professionally and personally.

18. You won't receive payments for unsocial hours.
19. You'll have fewer opportunities for training.
20. You'll have more stress because of increased responsibilities.

Hold on ... aren't these two lists contradictory? Yes they are! It's all contradictory – but it's all true. Running your own business is what you make it. And, to make it a success, you need to remember the three most important rules of working for yourself.

1. You must be permanently positive in public.
2. You must always think flexibly and laterally.
3. You must remember that, like a politician, you are never off duty.

HAVE YOU GOT THE RIGHT ATTITUDE?

I run a couple of newspapers. What do you do?

Orson Welles in his film *Citizen Kane*

An employee of a television company bumped into a former colleague, a television producer who had been made redundant a year earlier. The redundant man still saw himself as just that – redundant, without a 'proper' job, someone who had lost his status in the 'real' employment race.

He had, in fact, set up an independent television production company with other former colleagues. This company was now very successful in the field of media training for business people and the man himself had established a new full-time career based mainly on training. But he didn't see it like that; he thought that because he was no longer a full-time television journalist he wasn't doing anything worth mentioning.

When his former colleague asked 'What are you doing now?' he replied limply, 'Oh, you know, just bits and pieces'. And that was it. He didn't sell himself or his company. He automatically assumed the other man would look down on what he was doing, so he gave the impression that he was still waiting for someone to rescue him from working for himself by offering him a 'proper' job.

The moral of this story is to remember that the world doesn't give you your status. You must give yourself status. You must blow your own trumpet, particularly when you work for yourself. Then you'll knock the walls down.

Tie a knot and carry on

The Duke of Wellington said that Napoleon's army was very impressive with its smart uniforms and matching harness for all the horses. This he contrasted sharply with the British army, which he described as a rabble without proper uniforms and equipment.

However, the Iron Duke believed that Napoleon had gone too far with neatness and order so that the untidy business of real warfare was too much for his forces, and they were unable to proceed without the correct equipment. By contrast, his British 'rabble' were so untidy in the first place that if anything was broken or damaged they just tied a knot and carried on.

Wellington beat Napoleon.

The moral of this story is to remember that working for yourself means flexibility, positive thinking, tying and untying knots, cutting through problems and always working where you are, not where you think you ought to be according to a rigid fixed plan. Throughout this book there are examples of people doing exactly that and working successfully as a result.

Believing in yourself

It has been said – probably by a pessimist – that an optimist is someone who doesn't have all the facts. However, just who *does* have the full picture – all the time – on everything? It's this pessimistic type of 'can't do' attitude that gets people into the 'If I can't write plays as well as Shakespeare, I won't write anything' line of thinking. You could just as easily say that a pessimist is someone who knows a lot but never does anything about any of it.

Working for yourself means believing in yourself. It's all about:

self-assertion	making your points firmly, clearly and concisely
self-belief	trusting your own instincts
self-confidence	believing in yourself and your chosen line of work
self-esteem	believing in yourself and taking yourself seriously
self-help	getting used to relying on your own judgements
self-image	smartening up mentally and projecting that confidence in a smart appearance consistent with your role
self-improvement	learning constantly and building on failures as well as successes
self-reliance	trusting your own judgements and keeping a grip on reality
self-sacrifice	being prepared to work long hours
self-starting	believing in your own ideas, listening to customers, being open to new ideas and going for new business – not just thinking about it

Self-starters turn ideas into action. Take Kenneth Branagh and Emma Thompson: in a recent magazine feature about the award winning actor/director and actress, a friend was reported as saying that both of them had the shortest space between ideas and action of anyone he had ever met. In other words, if they have an idea they think is a good one, they go for it, work at it and do it. That's what *you* need to do to keep ahead of the game.

Still undecided?

There are many more ambitious people around than there used to be. Twenty-five years ago, when I started work, people had low sights; they just wanted a job provided by someone else and they were happy even if the money wasn't too hot. We were all brought up to know our place and not to question too much or even think of developing a career. Nowadays, people want more out of life, and setting up their own businesses enables them to get on further and faster.

Dennis Walsh, builder

Are you still unsure whether working for yourself is for you? The following questionnaire should help.

Part 1   IS THIS YOU?

		Agree	*Disagree*
1.	I love office politics	❏	❏
2.	I enjoy sniping at the boss	❏	❏
3.	I enjoy sniping at the organisation I work for	❏	❏
4.	I enjoy having a boss	❏	❏
5.	I think winning at work is fiddling my expenses	❏	❏
6.	I don't want to get up earlier than usual to make a deal	❏	❏
7.	I like to plan my holidays at least six months ahead	❏	❏
8.	I like routines in all my work	❏	❏
9.	I hate cancelling or changing personal appointments	❏	❏
10.	I hate cancelling or changing professional appointments	❏	❏
11.	I never want to discuss money	❏	❏
12.	I hate making deals	❏	❏
13.	I hate working under pressure	❏	❏
14.	I think an assistant should always answer my phone	❏	❏
15.	I don't want to discuss business in the evenings	❏	❏
16.	I don't want to work at weekends	❏	❏
17.	I don't like taking quick decisions	❏	❏
18.	I don't like responsibility	❏	❏
19.	I want to do the same thing every day	❏	❏
20.	I want to pass the buck	❏	❏

21. I don't want to have to look for my work ❑   ❑
22. I want security of employment ❑   ❑
23. I want an ordered social life ❑   ❑
24. I want a social life without discussing ❑   ❑
    business
25. I am not prepared to take a drop in ❑   ❑
    income

Not the time to change?

If you **agree** with **10 or more** of these questions, you could find it very hard to work on your own. Look again carefully at your answers, and decide whether you're prepared to try and change your attitudes to work, or whether you would really be happier working for someone else. Try Part 2 of the questionnaire and see how you get on.

Ready for change?

If you **disagree** with **15 or more** of these questions, you may have some of the right attitudes that will help you succeed. But even if you disagree with all 25 statements, don't get too confident. Try Part 2 of the questionnaire and answer truthfully.

No choice?

If you *have* to work for yourself, whether you want to or not, don't worry about your result. Read Part 2 of the questionnaire, look at your result, then study the questions carefully. Because if you have no option but to earn your living working for yourself, these are the work attitudes that will help you to survive and even to succeed.

Part 2   CAN YOU SAY YES TO . . . ?

                                             Yes   *No*

1. I want to be my own boss ❑   ❑
2. I don't like working for other people all ❑   ❑
   the time

3. I want responsibility for my own income ☐   ☐
4. I really enjoy making deals ☐   ☐
5. I can discuss prices and fees without blushing ☐   ☐
6. I can find the bottom line ☐   ☐
7. I like working under pressure ☐   ☐
8. I am hungry for work ☐   ☐
9. I want to do something different every day ☐   ☐
10. I want to work until a task is finished ☐   ☐
11. I don't want to plan my social life weeks ahead ☐   ☐
12. I don't expect every weekend off ☐   ☐
13. I enjoy working long hours ☐   ☐
14. I want to create my own job ☐   ☐
15. I want to learn every day ☐   ☐
16. I don't mind coping with anything ☐   ☐
17. I can set priorities ☐   ☐
18. I can hire and fire other people ☐   ☐
19. I can think on my feet ☐   ☐
20. I never want to turn down work ☐   ☐
21. I enjoy solving problems ☐   ☐
22. I think the buck stops with me ☐   ☐
23. I am confident in my own abilities ☐   ☐
24. I listen to my clients ☐   ☐
25. I like new ideas ☐   ☐
26. I like professional gossip and networking ☐   ☐

Still not ready?

If you have **more no than yes answers**, you are likely to find working for yourself very hard because you have such rigid mental attitudes to work. The first thing you must understand about working for yourself is that your time is your money. If you have to work at weekends or take phone calls in the evenings, it's not because anyone is imposing on you – it's because you need to, for the sake of your own income and you are choosing to do this for your own advantage.

Ready, steady, go?

Just being able to swim doesn't mean you can compete in the Olympics. **More yes than no answers** only means you're in training for the big event of running your own show; it doesn't mean you've solved everything. But it does give you a good base on which to build.

Still no choice?

Lots of no answers, but still have to jump in the pool however cold the water seems to you? Start the process of change now. Work on yourself. Mental exercise can be as valuable as physical exercise in making you fit for self-employment. If you resent being forced to work outside an organisation and having to think on your feet on a wide variety of topics, ask yourself, 'Who am I working for? What's the advantage in working hard? Who gets the benefits?' There's only one answer – you and your clients.

Self-employment means working *on* yourself as well as working *for* yourself. Believing in what you do is half the battle won.

CASE HISTORY:

The Long-distance Piano Man

Subject	Peter Juniper
Current role	Piano tuner and technician
Nature of business	Piano tuning and repairing
Location	Near Bude, Cornwall and in North London
Hours worked	48 a week, plus travelling

Number of employees	Just Peter
Turnover	£20,000 a year
Advertising/ marketing	Word of mouth, plus some local advertising in North London, newspapers and *Yellow Pages*

IT'S 235 MILES EXACTLY from Peter Juniper's cottage with its three-quarters of an acre of land near Bude in Cornwall to North London, where he has his piano tuning business. His wife and three teenage children live in Cornwall, while he stays with his wife's mother four days a week and works in London.

'You have to go where the work is, and obviously there's more work in London than in outlying areas like Cornwall,' he says. 'I've got established customers in London, and although I'm now building up some customers in Cornwall, there just isn't the volume of work around to justify being there all week. We wanted a country upbringing for the kids, and it's been much better for them than staying in London. Some people might think it's a bit daunting doing all this travelling, but I don't mind it too much.'

Peter used to have a piano shop and workshop in North London, but the rent and business rates became a real drain on the business. So, after 15 years of trading, he closed the shop and for the past 5 years has been a long-distance commuter. The journey usually takes him four-and-a-half hours by car, though it's quicker at night when there's not much traffic.

'Ideally, I'd like to spend three weeks in London and one week in Cornwall, then move to half and half – two weeks in each place. That would be more cost effective, too, because at the moment it's costing me at least £60 a week just for the travelling. But being flexible is essential when you run your own business. There was no way I was going to give up my business just because the shop rents and the business rates went sky high.

'I usually work from 7.30 a.m. to 7 p.m., four days a week. But I like my work, and I'm in charge of my own hours, so there's a lot less pressure than if I were working for someone else and travelling a long distance every week.'

Q. *What's the best and the worst thing about being self-employed?*

A. The best thing is being your own boss and being free to make your own decisions. The worst thing is no paid holidays. If you don't work you don't earn any money, so you tend to get up earlier and work longer hours to make up.

Q. *What advice would you give to others?*

A. You have to do your homework and be as well prepared as you can before you start. Be aware of all the expenses you're taking on, especially if you're taking premises. Try and be sure you can generate enough work to pay the bills. Get your stationery prepared, and be ready to advertise and market yourself. Not everyone can be self-employed. Not everyone wants the responsibility. You have to be self-disciplined. Even if you don't feel like it, you get up and get on with the work. So you have to like what you're doing, and be confident in yourself and your skills. If you don't like what you do, you won't be able to stick at it. Even if you're forced into working for yourself because you lose a job, you must find something that relates to your skills and what you like doing.

WHAT ELSE WILL YOU NEED TO GO IT ALONE?

Flexibility

You will need to be mentally flexible – that is, prepared to consider all available options before you make a decision. This is particularly important if, at first glance, the answer to any question seems to be 'No'.

Saying 'No' – do's and don'ts

- If the work is in your field, you must never say no immediately and without thinking. Instead, say 'I'll call you back in five minutes', then think hard and flexibly about new methods or new rates of charging – and ask someone else for advice if necessary – then ring back with a clear decision.

- You must never turn something down just because you've never been asked to do it before. On the other hand, you should not take something on just because it's offered. It could be too much if it's completely new to you.
- You should always think clearly: what are the pros and cons? Is this deal worth it in terms of time and money?
- If you do have to turn something down, you'll need to consider whether you still help the client – for instance, by recommending someone else not in competition with you to do the job or naming a contact who can recommend someone to take on the work. In other words, can you give the client a lead and keep them thinking you're still useful to them, even if you can't help directly in this instance?

Organisation

You won't have to do absolutely everything yourself; in fact, you can't – you're unlikely to have the time or expertise. Organisation is about working out what you can do and what someone else can do better. For instance, you'll certainly need an accountant to deal with your tax returns, possibly a part-time book-keeper and maybe even someone to do some of the day-to-day paperwork – who could be your husband, wife or partner, say, one day a week.

Just one small regular input of someone else's time can be worth far more to you than what you pay them. If someone else can do in a morning what might take you a day or even two days, you'll have saved money by paying them a fee.

So think about whether you'll need a secretary or assistant when you start. If so, will you need him or her to work full-time or just part-time? You could, for instance, employ someone just one morning or afternoon to begin with and see how you go.

It may be difficult at first for your business to afford salaries for two people, or even one-and-a-half. In this case, you'll be right to manage on your own. On the other hand, it might be false economy if, without help, you could lose business by not responding to clients and enquiries quickly and efficiently. It's a judgement *you'll* need to calculate and make.

Persistence and determination

These are the two qualities recommended by Ray Kroc, the man who built the McDonald's fast food restaurants into a worldwide success story. His advice is still handed out to McDonald's employees, and it's worth studying in the freelance and self-employed context:

> *Press on. Nothing in the world can take the place of persistence. Talent will not; nothing is more common than unsuccessful men with talent. Genius will not; unrewarded genius is almost a proverb. Education will not; the world is full of educated derelicts. Persistence and determination alone are omnipotent.*

Just make sure you persist in the right direction. Barking up the wrong tree in a dead-end street may just be a waste of time, no matter how much effort you give it.

Physical fitness

Keeping fit is not a luxury if you are working on your own. Even if you walk for just 15 minutes twice a day, you will be leaner and fitter than if you sit in the office or in the car all day and don't use your legs. If you can take some form of regular exercise – whether it's walking, running, swimming, playing tennis, squash or badminton, joining classes for aerobics, yoga or the martial arts – you will feel the benefits every day.

Everyone who is self-employed is under stress and stress without fitness can lead to serious health problems. Stress without fitness can also lead to tired, run-down people without the reserves to cope with long working hours and the pressures of constant decision making.

Not keeping fit could cost you contracts and contacts if you're not sufficiently on the ball to spot openings or stitch-ups when they arise. It can also mean you reach the end of your tether sooner than a fitter person, and start shouting and being angry when you should be thinking clearly.

Keeping fit also builds your stamina and without stamina you will find it very hard to get enough done, to keep going that extra mile when you have to, and still get up the next morning and be fresh enough to tackle another set of problems. Keeping fit makes it easier for you to have the stamina to cope with travel if you have to – particularly travel which takes you away from home overnight or abroad.

When you're an entrepreneur, you need to look successful. You have to have clear eyes and skin, plus energy and vitality. When you walk through a door, the first impression should be of your energy, and fitness gives that to you. If you walk into a room panting, and slump into a chair, you're not going to get the order or the contract, or even a day's work. Someone who is energetic gives the impression of more value for money. Someone who is lethargic and slow will give the impression that they think slower than average, and you begin to think you'll be paying them just to breathe.

Mary Spillane, CMB Image Consultants

I sit around a lot because I'm a writer. Being locked on the keyboard is not good for the brain or the hips so I swim regularly and I go to a stretch workout class twice a week. Going to classes doesn't just keep you fit, it stimulates your mind, and keeps you in touch with the real world and real people. If you work on your own, you really need to make contact with others, to keep your confidence up and to get things in proportion.

Deanna Maclaren, journalist and author

Mental fitness

When you are your business, part of the deal is selling yourself – probably every day in some way or another. Whether you are ringing up potential clients trying to get work or negotiating deals with people who have decided they want your services, you are having to put yourself on the line to generate your income, so you must develop your own ways both of projecting yourself professionally and protecting yourself personally against setbacks.

Some people have a natural ability to bounce along – ringing people up all the time and genuinely not noticing the rejections they suffer when others don't buy their services. Others are much more thin-skinned, with apparently very little defence against rejection; these people take every rebuff personally, and fall into dejection and depression whenever they get turned down.

However, although it is very important to take on board the message that 'you are your business', it is also important to understand that, logically, this does not mean that your business is you. Even if you are a one-person business, it is not you, with your spots, bald patch, back problem or personal insecurities, that the client is buying – it is your skills, knowledge and contacts that they want to pay for.

Yes, you are attached to your business self, and your business image is vital to maintaining your professional status and income. But a certain amount of detachment is necessary, in fact essential, to remain sane.

The key message is they haven't rejected you personally, but your business self – and, even when you're working on your own, that shouldn't be every bit of you.

Attachment and detachment

The Hindu religion has a concept of non-attachment. It's the ability to be attached enough to something to want to do it and to do it well, but at the same time not to be personally attached so that failure diminishes or damages you. It's also the ability to let things go, even when you've put a lot of time and effort into them.

This is the kind of thing that gets easier to manage as you get older and less self-conscious, and with a broader perspective on life in general. Young people find it hard to believe that when something they've worked on very hard is rejected, the rejection is not personal nor serious – even though sometimes it feels devastatingly so.

When older, more experienced people get the same treatment,

they can bounce back quicker and offer an alternative to the plan that's been turned down – and even turn a disaster into a triumph, if they can react quickly enough.

This is all part of a professional attitude whether you're self-employed or employed. But when you're working on your own, you may have no one else to fall back on if a client rejects something they had previously been keen on. You will have to think on your feet. And part of thinking on your feet is good preparation and having a few more ideas up your sleeve just in case your wonderful proposal is suddenly rejected.

There is never only one way to solve a problem. The perfect solution is what works *at the time*.

Support

Many people get valuable support from their partners and close friends. But not everyone finds a sunny, flower-strewn path opening up before them when they start to work for themselves.

Is your husband/wife/partner/parent/other close relative willing to lend you a hand? If they are, how much of a hand? If not, why not, and what are the motives behind their attitude to you working on your own business?

'If you really believe in yourself, you must accept that other people want you to fail,' says Mary Spillane of CMB Image Consultants. 'Even your partner, even your family, even your best friends. Because they don't want you to change. They fear your success because they think it will change you, and they don't want change. So people you thought you could rely on may not be sympathetic at all, which may come as a nasty surprise. If you're determined to succeed in spite of everything and everyone, you've got to have strong reserves inside, and be prepared to draw on them.'

WHEN OPPORTUNITY KNOCKS, CAN YOU HEAR IT?

The only place where success comes before work is in the dictionary

Vidal Sassoon

However many facts you know about setting up a business, however deeply you've looked into the legal and financial details, you won't be able to make the most of your own business unless you can hear opportunity when it knocks on your door.

One person may get a phone call out of the blue asking for a product or service which isn't in their normal range of business and may turn it down straight away without a second thought. Another person in the same situation may either think on their feet and offer a deal straight away or ask for the details and tell the potential customer they'll get back to them with a proposal for a deal. This person will work like mad to get something new set up and make sure they ring back at the time they agreed.

Even if things don't work out, they have used the time to find out facts that will be useful in the future. They've also established a helpful and positive image with a potential customer, who may talk to other potential customers about them in a positive way.

If you were in this situation – what would *you* do?

Finally, it can be very useful to write down all the queries you get out of the blue about things outside the mainstream of your business and look at these once a month or once a quarter, depending on how many queries you get. Think about the queries and decide whether there are new opportunities around that you haven't taken into account before.

CASE HISTORY:

Selling Sand to the Arabs

Subject	Ted Bonner
Current role	Sole trader – 'so I'm managing director, salesman, typist, secretary, telephonist and cleaner' – E.G. Exports
Nature of business	Exporting silica sand used for water treatment to the Middle East, plus water filters, heaters, and other electrical and electronic equipment
Location	Caunsall, near Kidderminster, Hereford and Worcester
Hours worked	Seven days a week, starting early in the morning because phone calls to the Middle East are cheaper before 8 a.m.
Employees	Just Ted, though his wife sometimes helps out with typing
Turnover	£130,000 in the first year of trading
Advertising/ marketing	Ted Bonner started off in 1992 with one client. Now has 13, in four different countries. Travels to the Middle East three or four times a year to make new contacts and renew old ones. Runs an advertisement in an English langugue daily newspaper, the *Khaleej Times*, which circulates in Dubai, Bahrain and Oman, for four days before he arrives. It states what he does, when he'll be arriving and where he'll be based. Last time he arrived at 6 a.m., got into bed in the hotel and the phone started ringing at 8.30. He gets plenty of enquiries.

YOU'VE HEARD of taking coals to Newcastle or selling ice-cream to the Eskimos? Well, now meet the man who sells sand to the Arabs.

Ted Bonner, a civil engineer by training, started selling British sand to customers in the Middle East when he returned to Britain in 1992 after several years working for a swimming pool company in Oman. The special silica sand, which he ships out in container loads supplied by companies in Leighton Buzzard and Stoke-on-Trent, is used for water treatment in desalination plants, sewage works and swimming pools.

Desert sand is not the right sort of sand for water treatment and silica sand has to be imported to the Middle East, a market opportunity that Ted Bonner is finding provides a steady income.

He also exports electrical and electronic equipment, including water filters and heaters. One order for 450 heaters for Bahrain, was, he explains, not at all mystifying in a country where temperatures frequently reach 40°C because, in the winter, temperatures can drop to as low as 15°C. This may sound like an average summer day in Scunthorpe but, as Ted points out, if you're used to very high temperatures, 15°C feels cold.

'I get a variety of requests on top of the business linked to sand and water treatment,' he adds. 'I've been asked for heaters, radiators, fencing, even doorknobs, and I'm trading now with companies in Oman, Dubai, Bahrain and Sharjah. When I was last out in the Middle East I even had one request for three million pounds' worth of scrap metal.'

'Why did I become self-employed? I wrote for 70 jobs and I had 1 interview. I did work for agencies as a freelance civil engineer, and was getting colossally well paid by the hour or by the day for doing work I'd done years before for a pittance as a beginner. It was straightforward stuff, doing surveys and setting out – that's laying out the lines, often with peg and string, sometimes with lasers, that the builders will work to on site. Then, out of the blue, I had a phone call from a colleague in the swimming pool firm I'd worked for in Oman. He said he needed someone to supply him with equipment. I thought "If I can supply him, I can supply anyone", and that's how I started.'

In fact, Ted started his business by hardboarding his attic and putting his desk and computer into a small space he had to climb a loft ladder to reach. Now he works at home in a spare bedroom and is a classic 1990s business, relying on fax and phone to keep him in touch with the world.

He's an example of translating opportunity, necessity and an existing knowledge base into a successful new business.

Q. What are the best and worst things about being self-employed?

A. The best things are no travelling to and from work, being my own boss, and having fewer worries and frustrations than when I worked for someone else. Also, I do enjoy my work.

The worst is having to rely on British manufacturers, some of whom are often inefficient and slow. For instance, I had an order recently for 2500m of fencing for a stadium in Oman. This was on a Friday and they wanted estimates of costs by the following Monday. I told them this would be too difficult and they extended the deadline to a week. I rang four companies and they all said they'd send quotes, but not one of them did within the week, so I had to fax an apology. Ridiculous isn't it?

I'm also not very happy about my bank, which makes it difficult for me to open accounts in other currencies. It took the staff a week to ring me back after I told them I wanted an account in Italian lire. Then the bank charges me £75 per cheque drawn on that account. Is that really fair? Is it good for trade?

Q. How do you see the future?

A. I feel that if people can see an opening they should go for it. As long as you've got the determination and the will to put in a lot of effort, it will pay off.

Q. What advice would you give to others?

A. Join a business organisation. I joined the Birmingham Chamber of Commerce and it's been very useful indeed. If someone asks me for a product I've never supplied before, I just ring up the Chamber of Commerce and they put me in touch with some useful contacts or they fax me information from handbooks with lists of possible contacts. Before I became a member, I used to spend hours in the library looking for information and I wasted a lot of time.

Take the Streisand approach

Throughout the book you will find advice telling you to go and find an expert on the particular issue you need to know about and get their input. But how do you find these people? And why is it that some people always seem to know someone to solve a problem for them, while others flounder about trying to do things themselves and getting nowhere fast? There are guidelines you can follow if you need to find a bookkeeper, accountant, solicitor, insurance agent, office cleaner, part-time secretary, computer expert, estate agent, childminder, plumber, despatch rider, printer, supplier, retailer, business partner and so on.

Just keep in mind the title of a song sung by Barbara Streisand called 'People who need People'. Anyone generating their own income directly as a freelance or self-employed person running their own business *always* needs people. If you think you can do it entirely on your own, you're going to make things much harder for yourself than they already are. I belong to NETWORK, one of the many voluntary organisations for professional women, which provide social and business contacts for women who wouldn't otherwise meet. One of our slogans is 'I may not know how to do that, but I know a woman who does'. And it works. It works for the millions of people who belong to professional trade, or social groups.

The more people you know, the more resources you have when something comes up which needs detailed skill or expertise which you just don't have yourself. Working for yourself is difficult and complex enough without wasting time trying to do things you're not trained for which will probably take you ten times as long to do as a person trained to do it, and you may also make mistakes while you're wasting your own valuable time.

Become a collector of useful people. Remember who told you about so and so who's an expert on importing and exporting, or isn't whatshername's brother a lawyer specialising in employment contracts, or what was that article in the paper about a woman who provides a bookkeeping service? People are a valuable resource and you should pile them up like gold bars in a vault. Contacts can be the difference between keeping going and going under. Even if one person can't help you directly they can give you the name of someone else who can.

Even if you don't know anyone remotely useful, you can always try a trade or professional organisation. If you ring the wrong one, they can put you on to the right one. If you don't know where to start, ring up or go to your local library and ask for the Directory of Organisations. This has lists of hundreds of groups and organisations. Or try your local Citizens' Advice Bureau or Chamber of Commerce.

Whatever you do, don't sit on a complicated problem and hope it will go away. This may work in a very few cases but it's by no means a sound business method. Taking action and getting advice can cost money, but often the cost is a lot less than if you took no action at all.

People who need people – seven steps to success

RULE ONE – You can't do everything yourself

RULE TWO – You will always need to find people with expertise you can rely on

RULE THREE – Never be afraid to ask your friends and acquaintances for advice on useful people

RULE FOUR – Never be afraid to explore the possibility of joining social or professional networks and/or professional or trade organisations

RULE FIVE – Free advice can be good advice, but never be afraid to consider spending money on getting expert advice

RULE SIX – Never be afraid to ask obvious questions

RULE SEVEN – Re-read rule one

2

Capitalising on Your Ideas and Skills

—•—

Imagination is more important than knowledge

Albert Einstein, scientist

YOU ARE YOUR BUSINESS

HOW DO YOU get from a staff job or from a period of unemployment to working for yourself? Whether you are pushed or whether you jump into self-employment of your own free will, it sometimes seems an impossible task to imagine yourself running your own show. Some people have definite ideas about the kind of work they want to do and the kind of product or service they want to offer; others are unsure what to do, where to look for ideas and how to start thinking about the issue at all.

One way to tackle the problem relating to work and career progression is to list your assets and interests as though you yourself were a business. Treat yourself like a small business, and analyse your professional advantages and disadvantages, your assets in terms of skills and experience, and your present and potential markets. Analyse your past and present. Project your future plans. Use the guidelines in this chapter to help you sort out your aims and aspirations.

Your personal and professional assets

The following exercises may take you 10 minutes to do. They *should* take you longer – at least half an hour – if you think things through thoroughly and carefully, and explore every aspect of what you come up with.

Take four sheets of A4 paper. Use **page 1** to list your personal and professional plus points. Divide the page into three sections:

1. **Exams, tests and trophies.** Write down all the exams you have passed, including driving test. Add sport, martial arts, music or dance qualifications, or trophies, any other hobby qualifications, including certificates of proficiency in First Aid, or certificates you have gained at work. Then write down which of these you enjoy doing most. You can write more than one interest if you wish. These are your **achievements.**

2. **Jobs undertaken, paid and unpaid.** List each of these in date order, with the official title of job – for instance: office assistant; shop assistant; junior secretary; secretary to sales manager; mother caring for baby; gardener at home; school governor; secretary etc. This is your **career progression**, and will give you an idea of how your life is moving and what skills you are acquiring.

3. **Hobbies and interests.** Write down how you spend your spare time when you have any. Then write down which of these pastimes you are most interested in and which you could consider using or would like to use in your work. Think carefully about everything you've written down. Have you forgotten anything? Now think about what skills you use to do these jobs. These are your **non-work skills and knowledge.**

On **page 2** you are going to take your plus points further. Divide **page 2** into three sections:

1. **Skills you already use.** List your skills – what you actually did, or do, in all the jobs you have done. For instance, answering the phone, taking messages, sending and receiving faxes, keeping a diary, filing, word processing, feeding paper into the photocopier, organising maintenance of the photocopier and other office equipment, organising post and dispatch riders for urgent

deliveries, organising meetings, taking minutes of meetings, organising temporary secretaries, directing the work of office juniors, organising petty cash, driving etc.

2. **Skills you are best at.** List the things you think you are best at in your job.

3. **Skills you are not using.** List any things you think you are good at which you are not using in your job, plus any skills you need to improve.

On **page 3** you are going to write down your likes and dislikes. Divide **page 3** into three sections:

1. **Work dislikes.** List all the things you most dislike about any of the jobs you do or have done. For instance, 'I dislike having to be on time', 'I hate working outdoors', 'I hate speaking in public', 'I do not like driving all day', 'I hate driving on motorways', 'I do not want to work with children'. Make your statements as definite as possible.

2. **Work likes.** List all the things you like doing when working or when pursuing interests or hobbies. For instance, 'I like adding up figures', 'I love driving on motorways', 'I like committees', 'I like chairing meetings' etc.

3. **My ideal job in my own business.** Based on all the things you like and dislike, and can or cannot do, put down a description of your ideal job in your own business and why you want to do it. This is not the time to say you want to be like J.R. Ewing in *Dallas* or Joan Collins in *Dynasty*. Put down something which is related in practical and skills terms to all the things you have written so far. For instance, if you are in sales, you might decide to start your own business using your selling techniques but with different products from the ones you're selling now, or you might want to train other sales people, or you might want to quit sales as such and work in an entirely different style. Your ideal work would then be related to, but not exactly the same as, what you are doing now. Look at your previous jobs, your hobbies, your interests. Is there a gap in the market for something in a field where you already have an interest?

Use **page 4** to write down what practical steps you can take in the future to get to your ideal. Writing down 'I plan to marry a millionaire/millionairess' is not necessarily helpful, unless you've already got advanced plans and contacts in that field.

Stick to what you *can* do and how you can do it. Ask yourself these questions.

- Are there people you could ask for advice?
- Will you need to take any more tests or exams?
- What are you going to do about getting more qualifications?
- What are you going to do about getting more experience?

List your assets, your aims and your plans to achieve those aims.

How to analyse the results

1. Put the four pieces of paper away for a week.
2. Fix a time when you are going to look at them again.
3. Come back to them, and see if you still feel they are accurate and useful.
4. Change them if you need to and add to them if you need to.
5. Rewrite your conclusions if you wish.
6. Continue thinking about your conclusions.
7. Start to act on them.

You may find you proceed in a completely different direction from what you expected. But, if it suits you and your skills, your character and your talents, then it will be right for you. Read the case studies in this book, looking at the career progressions of the people described. You can learn from what they have done.

Using your CV to get work

In the introduction to this book, I said that this is not a book for those who want other people to give them a full-time job. You might therefore think that your CV is not going to be relevant because you're not applying for jobs or turning up for job interviews clutching your neatly typed CV in your hopeful hand.

But CV's are not just for job applicants. They are also useful tools when you work for yourself. You are *not* applying for jobs, but you *are* frequently trying to convince people to give you work. In some businesses, for instance, journalism and broadcasting, freelance writers, camera operators, and technicians, are often asked to send their CV so that they can demonstrate their experience when applying for casual work paid by the day. In other business fields, as a freelance or a sub-contractor, your CV is not required in full, but you need to be able to use what what you know about yourself and your skills and experience to promote yourself and your business.

If you know your own CV, you can present your case for getting work very effectively to potential employers. If you're going to work for yourself you're going to be almost always on the lookout for work. Even when you're too busy to take on more work, you need to be thinking about how you will get the next assignment, contract or project. If you've worked for several different employers, you can use that to your advantage when talking to potential clients for your products or services, by pointing out that you have particular skills or background relevant to what they want. If you don't keep your CV at the front of your mind, you can all too easily find yourself in the frustrating position of putting the phone down at the end of a promising conversation and realising you didn't point out to the potential client that you have relevant experience which makes you exactly the right person for the work they want doing.

You need to know exactly what are your skills and experience so that you can promote yourself, whether on the phone or face to face, or in business letters, as the best person to supply services or products for that particular client. In addition, if you produce leaflets or brochures about your products or services, you will probably need to include something about yourself in the leaflet describing your career and emphasising your skills and range of experience in order to impress potential customers and secure yourself more work. It's easier to do this quickly if you have the information to hand to work on.

When writing your CV, always be positive and look at the best way of describing your work experience. Were you really 'Just a secretary'? Or were you 'providing secretarial support to the Personnel Manager, dealing with calls about confidential matters throughout the company, plus arranging her daily dairy, dealing with correspondence, and liaising with seminar and conference organisers'? Sounds a bit more interesting, doesn't it? If you can think positively about your previous experience, you can promote yourself successfully in your current role of working for yourself.

So you should always keep your CV up to date. Whether you use it in its entirety, or simply as a basis for a summary of your career, it's a resource you can return to and use time and time again as a basis for promoting yourself and getting work.

Forced into self-employment?

Most of the people I've interviewed for this book chose to take up self-employment, and when I asked what they would say are the best things about working alone, most mentioned words like 'freedom', 'personal choice', and 'independence'.

Interestingly, Tony King, the ex-mining electrician whose case history comes next, did not answer this question in the same way. Read his story, and you'll see that his reply is short and with a different perspective.

CASE HISTORY:

An Alarming Business Outside the Pit

Subject	Tony King
Current role	In charge of own one-man business, TWK Alarms, since mid-1993
Nature of business	Selling and installing security alarms for homes and shops
Location	His home in Wigan, Lancashire
Hours worked	'The wife says it's 24 hours a day. It's not quite that but, although I might be home at 9 p.m., I'm still thinking about things. I have to be flexible and work on Sundays or bank holidays if that's the only time the client can be there.'

Employees	Only Tony, though his wife takes telephone messages
Turnover	£35,000 p.a.
Advertising/ marketing	Local newspaper ads and publicity, plus word of mouth

SINCE HE WAS 16, Tony King had worked as a mine electrician, installing, maintaining and repairing mining equipment underground at the coalface. But in October 1992 his work dried up and the following March he was made redundant from the job he had relied on for 20 years.

That's when he decided to start his own business, selling and installing security alarms: 'I did the seminars, got my business plans together and set a goal of starting up on 1 May,' he says. 'And I did it.'

Tony put in a lot of research and hardwork, not only soaking up the free advice provided by British Coal Enterprise, which was set up by British Coal to provide advice and training for miners needing new jobs, but also writing his own business plan to help him get £40 a week for six months from the government's Enterprise Allowance Scheme.

He took and passed the City and Guilds examination to qualify him to deal with house wiring: 'In the mine you're working to the Mines and Quarries Act 1956. With houses it's the Institute of Electrical Engineering Wiring Regulations sixteenth edition. You're supposed to take a year of evening classes at college and then take the exam, but I did a week in the training centre with British Coal Enterprise and, a month later, I took the exam and passed it.'

He also went to free training seminars on book keeping, advertising and marketing, run by Wigan New Enterprise Limited and specifically aimed at people wanting to become self-employed.

His career change from employee working in a pit, to self-employed electrician installing alarms over a large region, took several months and has been 'quite a shock because it's a total change of work'. But, he says, it has its compensations: 'In the mine, I saw the same people and places every day. Now, I see different people every day. I see three-, four- and five-bedroomed houses all over the North West, and it's widened my horizons.'

Research has shown that only a minority of the miners made redundant in the 1980s have made a success of small businesses, and

some have tried to aim too high and lost all their money. Tony is
cautious and is taking one step at a time. He doesn't want to be a big
business.

'I don't want to expand the business beyond myself. You can fit an
alarm and you can fit an alarm — there's good ways and bad ways. I
set very high standards, so I'd have to train someone to my standards
and that would take too much time. Besides, I don't want to rely on
someone else. There is a lot of competition, but I've researched the
market thoroughly and I don't compete only on price; I compete on
quality. It's personal service, the quality of the job and reliability of the
equipment that I go on.'

**Q. *What are the best and worst things about being self-
employed?***

A. The best is no night shifts. And the worst is not having constant
work — being busy for one week or a fortnight and then waiting
for the phone to ring. It's hard, too, having no one to fall back
on.

It's good to be your own boss but it's a different sort of responsibility
to working for a big organisation like British Coal. If a problem occurs
in the mine, you can ask the supervisor for advice. Being on my own
means the buck stops with me. You've got to really know what you're
doing because, if there's a problem, who do you ask?

Q. *How do you see the future?*

A. I want to remain a one-man business and I want as much work
as possible without killing myself. I don't want to make a million,
I just want to make a decent living, and keep myself and my
family.

Q. *What advice would you give to others?*

A. Don't delve too deeply into things you don't need to know. For
instance, I went on courses about book keeping, which were
useful but were too complicated for me and my needs. Courses
can be very useful but you have to take what you need out of
them — you don't have to follow them completely.

I took another course run by British Coal Enterprise about dealing
with job interviews. I already knew I wanted to have my own business
— I wasn't going to get a job from someone else — but I still found it
useful because they were talking about selling yourself at interviews.
So I turned the interview technique into a sales technique. I learned
from the advice and adapted it for my own use.

THINKING CREATIVELY

Someone somewhere needs your services

Example 1: a company in the US is in the business of retrieving supermarket trolleys. It has 65 employees and a turnover of $3 million. It fills a gap in the market. It satisfies a need for big supermarket chains to get their trolleys back and it does this by charging only a dollar a trolley. If some American shoppers weren't so irresponsible, this company wouldn't have a business. But, then, if the world were perfect, a lot of people would be out of a job!

Example 2: famous for 15 minutes? Also in the US, there are now consultants who will train you how to react if you are stopped by a reporter in the street. People are paying out for this service, so it must have touched a real nerve in New York and Hollywood, where everyone would like to think they will be stopped, interviewed and featured in print, on radio, or on television as part of normal life: 'Yeah – I just *had* to take that course on how to deal with reporters – people always want to interview me. Don't you have that problem?'

Example 3: in Finland, a woman has made a very profitable business out of charging for looking after graves. She now has 130,000 graves to keep tidy. This example of enterprise in a usually quiet area of the economy has inspired a Gloucestershire couple to set up a similar service here. They've recognised a need, and a market, and approached their service very professionally.

Example 4: Rex Harden, now in his late 40s, had been made redundant in 1991 when he turned a chance remark by a friend about the difficulty of maintaining his relatives graves into a grave-tending business. He spotted the opportunity and in 1992 with his wife Fern, a florist, set up his aptly named business, Forget-Me-Not, caring for several hundred civilian and military graves in Gloucestershire, Worcestershire and Hampshire.

More good ideas

Say no to T-shirt printing?

In 1993, a survey of 1000 small businesses helped by the Prince's Youth Business Trust (PYBT) in the West Midlands showed that T-shirt printing, car valeting and fashion shops had the highest failure rates, with only around one in five still in business after a couple of years. However, all the florists and horticulturalists helped by the Trust, four out of five jewellery makers, 77 per cent of beauticians and mobile hairdressers, and 70 per cent of those designing and making clothes, were successful.

More than half of those working in painting and decorating, food and catering, hair salons, arts and crafts excluding jewellery, graphics and printing, sport and leisure, and theatrical and live performance, were also trading successfully. National surveys have shown that the PYBT, which provides grants and loans for young people aged 18 to 29 starting up businesses, has a success rate of two-thirds of businesses still trading after three years.

See page 106 for more information on the Prince's Youth Business Trust and the help it can give.

Lodgers can be tax free

If you have a spare bedroom or bedrooms, you may find it useful to explore the possibility of taking in lodgers and using the income from this as a way to pay some of your bills or to fund childcare while you are working.

The good news for would-be landlords and landladies is that money you earn from lodgers can be tax free. The current limit is £3250 per annum, a tax free allowance which has existed since April 1992. Below this limit, all your income from a lodger or lodgers is tax free. If your income is above the limit, it can be taxed normally as income or you can calculate your profit from letting – rent received minus your expenses – and be taxed on the profit.

A lodger is someone who rents a room from you, shares bath-room and kitchen facilities, and for whom you may provide some food, although you do not have to. The key point is that lodgers do not have self-contained accommodation. If they do, they can be classified legally as tenants and then they have legal rights of tenancy. Lodgers have no right to stay on in your home after the agreed period of their stay has ended or if you ask them to go. The Department of the Environment has clear and useful booklets for people with rooms to let in their homes: they recommend taking up references and making a clear agreement with any lodger about the exact terms of their stay with you, preferably in a written agreement.

Paying guests

If you want to go on any of the registers of accommodation provided to tourists by local tourist boards, you have to comply with the accommodation standards set by the tourist boards. Contact your local regional tourist board or the British Tourist Authority in London.

What about setting up an employment agency?

Secretaries, office cleaners, domestic cleaners, au pairs, nannies, nurses, carers, teachers, receptionists, office staff, hotel staff, com-puter programmers – these are just a few of the jobs now handled by employment agencies. The Federation of Recruitment and Employment Services (FRES) has 2500 licenced agencies in its membership.

Leonard Allen, formerly director of FRES and now a freelance consultant to a number of organisations, including FRES, says: 'If there's an occupation, there's no doubt an agency covering it. This federation started in 1930, when most employment agencies were for secretarial or domestic work. Now there's a vast range and enormous variety of agencies, from cleaners to headhunters, nan-nies to teachers.' FRES does not cover entertainment, theatrical and model agencies, dating agencies or escort services.

The Department of Employment is responsible for licensing private recruitment organisations and you cannot legally trade as an agency until your licence has been issued, which may take two to three months. When you apply for your licence you have to find suitable premises as the licence covers not just the individual, partners or limited company running the business, but the premises as well.

Running an employment agency from home could be difficult if you expect to have people regularly visiting you for assessment and you will also need planning permission from your local council. However, in the case of an au pair agency, it is not uncommon to get permission to run this from home. Few visits are involved, as the agency is purely an information link by phone, fax and letter between the au pairs who are abroad and the families who ring up to book them. For more information contact FRES – Checklist 4 for their address.

CASE HISTORY:

Vegetarian Visitors Need Aunties

Subject	Pauline Davies
Current role	Running and co-ordinating Aunties
Nature of business	Network of private homes and guest-houses offering accommodation for vegetarians coming to Britain as tourists
Location	Llanelli, Wales
Hours worked	Full-time office hours except in the winter
Employees	Just Pauline, but unpaid help from her husband
Turnover	Not disclosed

Advertising/	Produces a booklet every year called
marketing	'Vegetarian Visitor', 2000 of which are
	distributed by the British Tourist Authority in
	their offices abroad. In 1989, Pauline and her
	husband, Peter, were commissioned to
	compile *The Vegetarian Holiday and*
	Restaurant Guide to Britain. Pauline also
	travels to European countries two or three
	times a year, promoting her service.

PAULINE DAVIES has had a varied business career, including running
her own typesetting business in the US for several years during
her first marriage to an American. She started Aunties, an
accommodation service for tourists wanting to stay with British
families, in 1984.

At the time she was living with her second husband in Potters
Bar, just north of London, but they moved to Wales in 1989 when
he retired from his job at the headquarters of the Post Office in
Central London. 'Llanelli is my husband's home town, and it's
quite easy to run my business from here by phone and post,' she
says.

The original idea for Aunties came when a friend from the States
visited with her teenage daughter who told Pauline: 'Everyone should
have an Auntie in England like you.'

Spotting an opportunity for a small business, and having recruited a
dozen host families in North London, Pauline gave up her work for
the Citizens' Advice Bureau, obtained a grant from the Government's
Enterprise Allowance Scheme and set up in business. Within a year
she had 40 families on her books and had qualified for membership of
the London Tourist Board.

Aunties caters for all tastes, but began specialising in vegetarians
after an article in an American magazine, *Vegetarian Times*, brought
in a flood of enquiries. Pauline's market broadened to include tourists
from Europe and from other parts of Britain when the numbers
of American visitors to Britain were reduced by the Libyan crisis in
1986.

For Pauline, herself a vegetarian, Aunties is a way of life as well as
a small business, which suits her own international background. She
says: 'I don't have a huge turnover, but there are many other rewards.
We now have friends all over Britain and around the world, and

recently went to Moscow for a holiday at the invitation of Russian friends made through Aunties – we had a wonderful time.

'I've just started working with Environmental Travel, a new company based in the US which caters for vegetarians, vegans and people interested in animal rights. They're sending 200 people to London this year (1994) for an exhibition dealing with animal rights and environmental issues, and I'm organising accommodation for them. So I'm hopeful this type of business will grow in the future.'

Q. *What advice would you give to others?*
A. My first small business in Newark, Delaware, was a typesetting business for which I bought specialist equipment, which no one else in the town had, so that I could do fancy setting.

I had two big customers in the town. Unfortunately, because they were both big, they were also slow payers and this sunk the business in the end. I would ring up one of them and they would say, 'We pay alphabetically, paying so many people a week and we'll get to you in three weeks.' It was terrible.

So when I started Aunties, I made it a rule never to give credit.

FREE ADVICE AND SOURCES OF INFORMATION

Courses

Check out your local college – you may find a course to suit you. There are courses covering a wide variety of interests at colleges of further education and private colleges including catering, book keeping, upholstery, chimney sweeping, creative writing, yoga, Cordon Bleu cookery, hairdressing, beauty therapy, aromatherapy, foreign languages, floristry, photography and video production – to name just a few. If you can't find what you want at a local college, consult your library for information on private colleges and professional organisations running courses.

Check out your local library for general information on what courses are on offer in particular subjects and ask them for the brochures for local colleges.

Citizens' Advice Bureaux (CABx)

CABx provide the freelance or self-employed person with a free and informative sign-posting facility. They offer guidance on self-employment, starting a business, local authority help, government schemes and Training and Enterprise Councils (TECs) – see below. They can advise on choosing your business, how to register your business name, where to get financing and finding commercial property. Most boroughs, towns and cities have their own Citizens' Advice Bureaux, which are listed in *Yellow Pages*. They can also advise on bad debts, managing debts and how to use the Small Claims Court.

Training and Enterprise Councils

These are independently run local companies used by the Department of Employment to assess the employment needs of their own areas, and to run the training and business schemes which used to be run directly by the government. They can vary from area to area, but have five functions – encouraging employers to invest in training for their staff; youth training; career development; assisting the unemployed and disadvantaged into work; and providing education and training. Each TEC decides how these criteria can best be met in its own area.

Examples of different schemes include the following: South and East Cheshire TEC set up a special programme to train care assistants; Dudley TEC pioneered and engineered an apprentice scheme with local business support; LAWTEC, Lancashire Area West TEC, has opened an Opportunities for Women Centre offering career development loans and training; Tyneside TEC has started Freshstart, a training programme tailored for women returners; North Nottinghamshire TEC has various projects for women returners including 'Business through Enterprise' and 'Women into Management' – they also help finance childcare and travel expenses for women on these courses, and provide an information service, 'Careline', for people in work or hoping to return to work and needing to find childcare or care for dependent relatives.

Almost all TECs have business start-up schemes, and may offer grants to the unemployed to start up in business, and loans to those already in work but who want to start up on their own.

How do you find your TEC?

There are no standard names for TECs and no way of knowing what area each TEC covers, and whether you and your business are in one TEC or another. So contact your local JobCentre or Citizens' Advice Bureaux, and ask for the name and phone number of your local Training and Enterprise Council.

If you already have a business and your business address is different from your home address, your local TEC is the one covering the area where your business is situated.

In Scotland it's LECs

In Scotland, the functions of Training and Enterprise Councils are performed by Local Enterprise Companies, known as LECs. They provide a wide variety of information, advice, counselling and training services to small and large businesses, and cover help to businesses previously offered by the Scottish Development Agency and the Highlands and Islands Development Board. You can get information from the Scottish Office or your local JobCentre.

In Northern Ireland it's LEDU

In Northern Ireland the best place to get advice on starting up in business is LEDU – the Local Enterprise Development Unit. This is the Small Business Agency based in Belfast.

Yet more advice

Check out the careers section of your library for books on particular careers and small businesses. Ask for advice if you don't see anything relevant to your interests.

Research your market and assess the feasibility of your product or service. You need to set aside half an hour to concentrate on working out what leads to follow up to help you to decide whether what you want to offer really is a practical proposition.

Compare what you want to offer with what is already on offer in the same or a similar field. Who else is already in the same or similar line of business? Write them down. Ask yourself these questions.

- Am I offering the same service or product as others – if so, what makes mine different?
- Am I offering a different service or product from others – if so why has no one else done this before?
- Is my plan really practical or am I building on dreams and neglecting details?

Five questions to answer now in broad terms

1. What are my objectives?
2. What steps do I need to take to accomplish these objectives?
3. What money will I need to set up?
4. What money do I expect to make in the first year?
5. What advice do I need and where will I get it?

CASE HISTORY:

The Sweet Smell of Success

Subject	Ann Corsie
Current role	Sole proprietor of Reading School of Aromatherapy and Healing

Nature of business	Runs one-day workshops, two-day courses and a weekend course, as well as teaching evening classes in aromatherapy for Newbury Further Education College, and practising as an aromatherapist. Editor of *Aroma*, a quarterly scientific journal of essential oils, perfumery and aromatherapy
Location	Reading, Berkshire
Hours worked	At least 50 a week
Employees	2, plus freelance trainees as required
Turnover	Not disclosed
Advertising/ marketing	'I try things at regular intervals and continue them if they work and discontinue them if they don't. I use local papers – the *Reading Chronicle*, for instance, does supplements for business people – how to relax, how to get a massage, what aromatherapy is etc. – and you can sometimes have about 500 words of free editorial when placing an advert. I also advertise in *Here's Health* magazine every other month'

THE MOMENT you enter the kitchen of Ann Corsie's home in Reading, you notice there's something very unusual about it. It's not the exotic smells that linger in the air, it's the rows and rows of small, neatly labelled bottles on shelves covering one wall, and often covering the kitchen table as well. These are the 130 essential oils she uses in her work as an aromatherapist and aromatherapy teacher.

Aromatherapy uses aromatic or essential oils from plants and trees to achieve a state of balance and harmony in the human body, mind and spirit, and Ann took it up in 1990 – at first, working with a company selling oils, and now running her own school of aromatherapy.

There's another unusual thing about Ann – her face seems strangely familiar. This is because she starred in a long-running television commercial for Whiskas cat food in the mid-1980s, along with her cats and her then three-year-old son. She's not an actress – she was, and still is, a genuine buyer of the product; she just happened to meet the managing director of Pedigree Petfoods at a dinner and, two weeks later, was doing a screen test. So she's a person who both recognises opportunities and takes them – useful qualities when running your own business.

Ann worked as a shop assistant in a chemist's before training to be a geriatric nurse – a course she gave up when she married at 19. When she divorced at 21 she worked first as a beauty therapist, then as an executive for Tesco – training cashiers, book keepers and managers in office procedures. Then she ran her own very successful business for five years buying and selling original paintings. She had a concession of 500 ft^2 in Selfridges in London, plus her own gallery in Hoddesdon, Hertfordshire. 'Interestingly, the store used my venture as a test for the market for original paintings, because, after I left, they started running it directly for themselves.'

During her second marriage, she used her book keeping experiences to work with her husband in his import and export company. When that marriage failed, she spent 18 months as a director of a company that supplied aromatherapy oils. But after she trained as an aromatherapist, she decided to concentrate on teaching and practising the therapy.

'Aromatherapy is a holistic treatment,' she says. 'This means you are not just treating the symptoms but the whole person. It might be that people are emotionally distraught and you have to deal with their emotions as well as the physical symptoms. It deals with physical, mental and emotional health. In my practice, I use diet, meditation and relaxation techniques.'

Ann's skills lie in training, marketing and book keeping – all very useful for a small business with training as its core. Despite the New Age image of her chosen field, she does not dress in a hippy or flower-power peasant way; she looks mainstream, warm and friendly – all assets in gaining and retaining clients from a wide range of backgrounds. But, because she doesn't have a degree, at first she could only teach people about aromatherapy, not how to take an accredited exam in the subject. People with degrees can teach courses at further education colleges leading to exams, but people without degrees need to acquire teaching qualifications.

With her usual decisiveness Ann has now solved that problem. In the summer of 1994 she gained a teaching qualification – City and Guilds 730 – which qualifies her to teach exam-based courses. And since the autumn of 1994 she has been teaching the ITEC

(International Therapy Education Council) in anatomy, physiology and massage, plus a further diploma in aromatherapy. She offers her own internal Reading School of Aromatherapy qualification as well as the external courses and is aiming ultimately at full official accreditation for her own courses.

Ann is also a trained reflexologist, and a member of the National Federation of Spiritual Healers, and believes a healthy spirit and soul supports a healthy mind, which leads to a healthy body.

'Aromatherapy and massage go together, but it's only in recent years that massage has become more acceptable. Aromatherapy seems to have given it a respectability which was not there before. Touch is the sense which is frowned on in Britain. It's not like that on the Continent.

'Illness, smoking, alcohol – they can all have a cumulative effect on the body. It's probably taken a few years to bring about imbalance and illness, so it's likely to take time to encourage the body's own natural regenerative processes to restore balance and harmony.'

It's taken Ann Corsie many years to bring all her various skills together into one career, but she now feels she has found what she wants to do with the rest of her life – and, with her calm and calming manner and personality, she has both the talent and the will to succeed.

Q. *What mistakes did you make at the start?*
A. I'm still at the early stages, so I'm sure I'm still making masses of mistakes. My biggest failing is that I only like to do what I like to do and I'm no good at selling myself. I just want to treat people, give massages and teach classes, but I've got to go out and convince people that they need me. I keep putting it off because I hate doing it, but it's essential.

I've talked to other therapists and the therapy is what we do well – the selling is what we don't want to do. It is better now I can provide vocational training, not just training for people with an interest in the subject. As the school grows, I hope business will begin to roll naturally without so much need to market myself. As more people are taught, they will be my advertising.

Q. *What advice would you give to others?*
A. I think the make-or-break thing is commitment and belief in oneself. You must have total commitment, and positive belief and thinking, otherwise you'll give up. You will only manifest success

if you're convinced yourself. Nothing in this world ever happens without a thought. And, if it's a positive thought, you'll get a positive reaction. So, no matter how bad things seem, you have to remain positive.

3

Ideas Into Action

—■—

It is Enterprise which builds and improves the world's possessions . . . If Enterprise is afoot, Wealth accumulates, whatever may be happening to Thrift; and if Enterprise is asleep, Wealth decays, whatever Thrift may be doing.

John Maynard Keynes, economist

YOUR FIRST BUSINESS STEPS

YOU'VE GOT A GREAT IDEA. You feel you could be enterprising and turn it into a real business, but your head is spinning with possibilities and you don't know where to start. This chapter will give you a basic framework for getting your idea into its first shape. I say 'first shape' because you may find that what you start out with is not what you end up with when you start trading or working. But it's not the original idea alone that matters – it's how you marry that idea with reality, give it legs and start it walking, and in which direction, that will bring you your own successful business.

It's no use having a vague idea, carrying it around like a cloud and expecting it to turn into a sharp reality without doing any work on it to bring it down to earth. If you keep things cloudy, you're very likely to end up getting rain, not sunshine, at the end of the day. Yes, business people do need feelings and intuition about their businesses, and they don't have to define rationally every single action every second of every day, but they do need precision and method to pin down exactly what would be the best steps to take, and why.

In the last chapter, we looked at skills and abilities, and the resources you have within you. Now you need to assess and use those skills to write down exactly how you see things now and in the future. Once you have done this, you should find your plans becoming clearer and you may have to discard a few, some or all of your long-cherished ambitions. If you just want to dream, dream on – but if you want to set up your own business, now is the time to stop dreaming and get practical.

Your 'report to yourself'

This is not the same as your business plan – that comes later on, in the next chapter. Your report to yourself is your first step and is the spadework necessary to test out your theory of setting up on your own. It will give you the groundwork and get you into training, mentally, for preparing your business plan.

So often, people starting up on their own drift into situations which, with only a little planning and forethought, they could easily have seen would not be the best direction for them. Thinking things through is half the battle in business as in life. Of course, businesses can change shape at any time before they start, and again once they get going, because markets change, people change, ambitions change and new opportunities occur. But if you can start by thinking and planning logically, without resting on assumptions that may leave you in mid-air and in danger when you least expect it, you can give yourself much more chance of success.

My report: advice checklist

1. **Obvious questions.** Always ask them – you will need to do this every day when you are working for yourself, so start now. Don't be embarrassed about being obvious – you could be a lot more embarrassed if you don't ask and, later on, at a vital moment, you run out of a product, someone working for you leaves you in the lurch, a supplier closes down or a market dries up like the Sahara at midday.
2. **Doubts.** If you have a doubt, write it down. Then explore it, pursue it and nail it down. Never have a lingering doubt about anything you must rely on.
3. **Assumptions.** Never assume. You may assume you can get a

certain product, type of stationery or piece of equipment, because you always got it when you worked in a larger firm. But is that the reality? There may be special deals, for instance, discounts which you, as a new and small business, cannot get. Paying more will push up your prices.

4. **Details.** Always explore details if they are vital to your success. Don't get bogged down or take refuge in the safety of too much detail, but do decide which details you really need to know about your new business so you can sell it confidently to others.

5. **Intuition.** Learn how to assess your intuition, when to trust it and when to apply the above questions, doubts, assumptions and details. Also, learn when to trust or mistrust others on the same basis.

Writing your report

Take ten A4 sheets of paper and write the following heading at the top:

My business idea: a report by (your name)

followed by these ten headings at the top of each page:

Page 1   My idea
Page 2   My business
Page 3   My market
Page 4   My market opportunity
Page 5   My USP (unique selling proposition)
Page 6   My market research
Page 7   My business name
Page 8   My legal business shape
Page 9   My contacts
Page 10   My next steps – future action points

On each page it's useful to rule a line down the right-hand side to make a column about 4 cm wide. Head this column 'Action', and write in any action you need to take to progress your report, find out more etc.

On **page 10** you will write your future plans for your next steps as a result of your report to yourself.

Use the **checklist** above to question what you write on every page, so you are as rigorous as possible in planning to turn your dream into reality.

This report will give you your framework for future planning. It can be typed, handwritten or printed by a word processor, depending on your preference. You can set up and work directly on pages on your computer screen if that suits you best.

The main aim is to produce something easily legible which *you* can use for future reference. The report is not intended as a document to be read by others – it's for your use as your first step towards your own business.

My report: guidelines

Page 1: My idea
What is your business idea? Define it on paper. Will you be providing a service? Will you be producing a product? How do you describe your idea?

Example A: I want to set up a contract cleaning business offering cleaning services to offices. I will pick up the staff myself and drive the van to the offices with my own equipment in the early mornings. I will need to price my contracts competitively to attract business. I will be using cleaning equipment and a van five days a week. I will pay myself a salary and will be employing staff paid hourly.

Example B: I want to set up a business using my skills as a book keeper. I want to work from home, as well as travelling to see customers. I will offer a computerised service, and each customer will be a small business which will appreciate and value my personalised, highly efficient service.

Example C: I want to set up a business selling my own hand-made jewellery. I want to be based in a workshop which will also be a shop. I will need to employ someone to help me manufacture my jewellery, sell the products and run the shop. I think I will succeed because most of my jewellery will be fashionable and ethnic, and not too expensive to produce. I will also produce expensive one-off pieces which I will sell at high prices.

Page 2: My business

How will you develop your idea into your business? Write yourself a short report including the following.

- Your current work situation – are you still employed? Are you self-employed? Part-time? Full-time? Unemployed? If currently unemployed, can you get any extra help from government schemes?
- Possible premises – where are they? What do they cost? If working from home, what changes will be needed to create your working space?
- Possible staff required.
- Equipment needed.
- Finance needed. Do you need a loan or do you have enough capital?

Page 3: My market

- Do you have a new idea or are you joining an existing market?
- How secure is this market?
- Are there threats from new technologies?
- Will there be opportunities created by new technologies?
- What are the likely changes over the next five years?
- What are the likely changes over the next ten years?
- What have been the biggest changes in this market in the past ten years?
- Who are your likely customers?

Page 4: My market opportunity

- What is the gap in the market for you? Why do you think you can make an income in this market? What are your skills in this area?
- What gaps do your competitors leave?
- Are you looking for a gap in the market or a niche? Is it risky to go for niche marketing? A gap can be widened; a niche is narrow.

A niche is a small shelf in a church, or a formal room, usually intended for a special statue, vase or ornament. It does not have a broad horizon, but it can offer security and a place in the sunlight. However, it has limitations and there can be drawbacks.

When the fast-expanding Sock Shop hit hard times – particularly after a series of strikes on the London Underground (where many of its socks and tights shops were situated) badly dented its vital passing trade in London – the *Financial Times* carried an article headlined 'When a niche becomes a tomb'. If a market niche is too narrow it can stifle you, it can end overnight by coming to a dead stop or it can be filled in and the wall smoothed over so the niche simply doesn't exist any more. So it's as well to beware of basing your whole income on filling a tiny niche in a market.

Page 5: My USP (unique selling proposition)

What is your USP? What makes your product or service different? What do you have that your competitors don't?

If you can't think of a USP straight off, can you think of something you can use as a selling line for your business? Can you think of a slogan you would use to advertise your business?

Page 6: My market research

What is your preliminary market research? Analyse your competitors and survey your potential customers.

- Who are your competitors?
- Will they react against you?
- What will be your response or protection against competition?
- Is there competition from abroad?

Write yourself a short report.

Page 7: My business name

- What business names do you have in mind? Will your business name be catchy, informative or practical? What are your competitors called?
- Draw up three columns: 'Name', 'For' and 'Against'.
- Suggest some names.
- Write down for and against each name.
- Will you register your business name? You cannot trade under any name you feel like using. The use of some business names is

regulated by the Department of Trade. You can find out more by looking at Chapter 4 of this book and Checklist 2 at the end of the book.

Page 8: My legal business shape

No one can be enterprising and successful in business without some structure to shape the business around. Business structure doesn't have to be immensely complicated for a small enterprise, but it does have to be solid and definite, and clearly understood by the person or persons running the show.

The main categories of business are:

- sole trader;
- partnership;
- limited company;
- co-operative.

Any one of these may be the right one for you. There are advantages and disadvantages for each category, as you can see on pages 000–000 below. Get professional advice from your accountant or solicitor before deciding which is best for your business.

Page 9: My contacts

- Who do you know already in this market? Who do you know who knows someone who could be useful? Have you contacted any professional or trade organisations who may have useful information?
- Who do you know who can give you general business advice?
- Who do you know who could be your customers?
- Are you already a member of any clubs or groups where you have met, or can meet, people who may be useful to you?

Page 10: My next steps – future action points

What do you need to do next? Write down your future plans for your next steps as a result of your report to yourself.

Your next steps could be, for example:

- ring up friend of friend and arrange to talk in person or on the phone about a business issue or further contact;
- go to bank and get information on help for small businesses;

- make appointment to see Small Business Adviser;
- clear out spare bedroom/garage and turn into office;
- investigate office or workshop rents in area where the business should be set up.

If you have been able to make progress on your report to yourself and follow up your action points for the future, you are now ready to move on to drawing up your business plan. This is essential if you want to get a loan or a grant – you'll have to produce a business plan to convince those from whom you want to extract finance.

However, if you don't need any money from anyone else, do you really need to bother? In theory, the answer is no; in practice, it's yes, because the discipline of having to think through your ideas thoroughly can save you a lot of trouble in the future. It also means you start as you mean to go on – being businesslike and practical, not dreamy and hopeful, with assumptions and theories instead of facts and figures.

In the next chapter, we'll look at the detail of drawing up a business plan.

Points to watch

It is very important to work hard and not talk about it. We are often accused of being too discreet. But in the military you never say anything unless it is to mislead the enemy.

Alfred Schindler, chief executive of Schindler, the leading Swiss elevators and escalators group quoted in the *Financial Times*, 21 September 1993

Mind your own business

- Be careful – don't give anything away.
- Be discreet – discretion is the best policy.
- Trust no one – don't gamble your future on friends or acquaintances.
- Don't brag about your plans – transparency in business can be a big mistake.
- Don't sit on your idea – someone else may get there first.

Don't sit on things

Who invented the telephone? Alexander Graham Bell? Thomas Edison? A Russian scientist? All of them? The history of science and of business is littered with people coming up with and working on the same products or services at the same time.

If you can think of something, so can someone else. And while you're just contemplating the beauty of your great idea, polishing the possibilities and admiring your cleverness in spotting such a breathtakingly simple new product or service, others may be getting ahead of you by taking the whole thing further immediately and so getting to the market – and the money – first.

Even those with a flair for business don't catch every bus. Victor Kiam, the president of Remington ('I liked the shaver so much I bought the company'), who has built an extremely successful business career by anyone's standards, confesses in his autobiography that he missed one very big business opportunity. He was working for Playtex when an inventor showed him a new product he had devised. It was Velcro and Kiam immediately spotted its possibilities for bras. He took it to Playtex, but after several months they eventually turned it down and decided not to use it. Then he realised he should have thought less narrowly about a product which is now very widely used.

'It didn't occur to me at first to try to take this product out on my own,' he writes. 'Only after Playtex rejected it did I see the possibilities it held for me. It was too late. I should have entered a licensing agreement with my friend that would have allowed Playtex to use it for their products and permitted us to pursue other possibilities. I didn't see the opportunity. That was a tough lesson to learn. You can bet I didn't let many like that slip by me again.'

First man:	Where are you?
Second man:	In South America.
First man:	That's abroad isn't it?
Second man:	It all depends on where you're standing.

The Goon Show, BBC Radio

LEGAL BUSINESS STRUCTURE

Sole trader

Definition   One person trading under his or her own name or a business name

Advantages   No legal steps necessary to set up
You are taxed as as individual
Some tax advantages
You have total control over your business
You do not have to publish your accounts
Easy to wind up

Disadvantages   Has lower status than a limited company
You are responsible for all business losses
Your personal assets can be seized to pay debts

Summary

Sole trader is the easiest and simplest way for one person to go into business, but you must recognise that you will be self-employed and personally liable for losses. Your creditors can get court orders enabling them to seize your personal as well as your business possessions.

If you are thinking of setting up as a sole trader – **professional advice recommended.**

Partnership

Definition   Two or more people going into business together. Partnerships are often used in the professions, e.g. solicitors and accountants

Advantages   Has more status than a sole trader
No legal formalities
Some tax advantages

Two or more heads can be much better business than one
Less complicated than a limited company
You do not have to publish your accounts

Disadvantages

No legal structure
Risk of disagreements ruining the business
Legal costs of drawing up a partnership agreement
Raising funds may be difficult
Each partner is responsible for all debts
Your personal assets can be seized to pay debts

Summary

A partnership is not a formal legal structure, so it is simpler to form than a limited company. A partnership agreement is not a legal requirement, but it is usually advisable to draw up an agreement as, without it, a partnership can be very vulnerable to problems ranging from a partner taking too much time off, or too much money out of the bank, to a partner leaving and taking business or business assets with him.

If you are thinking of setting up a partnership – **legal advice essential.**

Partnership agreements – some guidelines

There is endless scope for disagreements between business partners but common areas of disagreement between partners include the following.

- How are major decisions taken? Do partners have votes?
- How many hours will each partner work?
- What holidays will be taken?
- How will you divide the profits?
- Who will sign the cheques? One or two people?
- What happens if a partner dies? Death automatically dissolves a partnership unless the partnership agreement states otherwise.
- What happens if a partner wants to leave?

- What notice of leaving has to be given?
- Can any new partners join the business?
- What system is there for settling disputes between partners?

These are just a few broad outlines of the potential problems. Your proposed business partners may be your best friends now and you may think they would never cheat you out of a cream cake, let alone a slice of a bank account. However, if things get tough – or even, conversely, if things get very prosperous – you may find they want to take a far larger slice of the gateau than you think is fair.

It is advisable to pay for legal advice when drawing up a partnership agreement. In a small partnership with only two or three partners, a partner leaving can be like a divorce. Who gets the car? The personal computer? The money? An agreement can reduce the traumatic and dramatic potential for those involved.

Limited company

Definition	A limited company has directors, whose liability to pay the company's debts is limited by law
Advantages	Higher status than sole trader Personal possessions cannot be seized to pay business debts Company legal identity is separate from shareholders Legal structure is well defined Capital can be raised by selling shares Bank loans may be easier to raise You are a company employee with a regular income
Disadvantages	More expensive to administer than a sole trader or partnership – not suitable for a small turnover Banks may ask for personal guarantees from directors Must publish accounts annually

Must file details of directors, company secretary and shareholders
You must be on PAYE, not Schedule D
You cannot borrow money from the company

Summary

A limited company has advantages over a partnership or a sole trader in terms of organisation and legal structure. The need to hold board meetings means directors have to explain their actions to each other and regular meetings can impose a useful business structure. However, it is not suitable or necessary for a small turnover since an accountant has to be paid to audit your accounts every year (and most people pay the accountant to draw up the accounts as well).

If you own and run a company, you have to be a director and you have to be paid as an employee. So, if you are already self-employed, you lose the advantages of Schedule D tax status when you become a company director. On the other hand, you gain the advantage of a fixed regular income. You should be aware that the protection of limited liability for business debts may be effectively removed by banks or other financial institutions, who have a nasty habit of demanding personal guarantees from company directors for loans to their companies.

If you are thinking of setting up your company – **professional advice essential.**

Legal requirements

Setting up a company is quite complicated and it is advisable to get it done by a professional person, such as a solicitor, an accountant or a company registration agent. A small business is a private limited company. A larger business is a plc – a public limited company.

A private limited company has to have a minimum of two shareholders. One director must be a shareholder. It must have a minimum of one director and a company secretary, who can be an outside person such as your accountant or solicitor.

A limited company has to be legally registered at Companies House, and before registration it must have a memorandum of association and articles of association. The memorandum sets out the main aims and objectives of the company; the articles of association set out rules by which the company will be governed. There are standard legal phrases for dealing with both these legal documents or, to put it another way, there is a lot of legal jargon involved, and it would not be sensible to try to tackle any of this without the help of a solicitor familiar with company law and procedures. A company cannot begin trading until it is issued with a Certificate of Incorporation and directors have been appointed.

Forming a company can be done from scratch, which is more expensive and time-consuming than the procedure many people follow of purchasing an 'off the shelf' company, i.e. a company which has already been registered, but which has no assets, is not trading and is offered for sale by a company registration agent. Once purchased, this ready-made company can be renamed by the new directors and registered under its new name, subject to checks under the laws governing registration of business names. Buying an 'off the shelf' company is faster and less expensive than setting up a company from scratch, but in some circumstances it may be necessary to set up your own company.

Every company has to have a registered office, which does not have to be the same address as the business address.

Business stationery

A company's business stationery must, by law, include the following details on letterheaded paper:

■ your full company name including the word 'limited';
■ your company registration number;
■ the country where the business is incorporated;
■ your registered office.

Check with your solicitor or accountant before you rush off and place a large printing order. If you use a different or shortened trading name and a trading address, you will have to give fuller details at the bottom of the page.

Invoices and statements must state your company VAT registration number, if you have one.

Co-operative

Definition   A business owned and controlled by all those working for it

Advantages   All employees can be given equal rights
Profits shared on the basis of contribution of work, not capital
Decisions are made democratically

Disadvantages   Too many people trying to run the business
Disagreements can arise over pay
Can't get decisions made swiftly enough
Too much time spent in democratic meetings
Can lose business focus

Summary

A co-operative cannot be run effectively unless everyone involved agrees with its aims and accepts the co-operative structure. This can be difficult to maintain in a society where most people accept and expect pay differentials, and regard different pay for different tasks as normal.

Co-operatives are often used by groups of people for purchasing in bulk – such as farmers buying supplies or families buying food from wholesalers. In these cases, the purpose of the co-operative is not income but the reduction of purchasing costs. The most famous example of co-operatives in business is the nationally known CWS, the Co-operative Wholesale Society, known colloquially as 'the Co-op' with its 'Divi' – the dividend and sharing out of profits among all who join.

If you are thinking of setting up a co-operative – **advice essential.**

YOUR FIRST BUSINESS STEPS – OTHER OPTIONS

Franchising

Franchising is a system in which a franchisor offers a ready-made, tried and tested business idea to a franchisee. The franchisor is the one who is selling a business concept and system to a franchisee, who pays for the use of a business idea which already works.

As a franchisee, you pay money up front and also money per year, or per month or per week (contracts vary) to the franchisor for the privilege of using their business idea to make money for yourself.

Franchising has grown steadily over the past 20 years in Britain and, according to the Brtitish Franchise Association, now provides 190,000 jobs; it even created 20,000 new jobs in 1993, when the British economy was still struggling with the effects of recession.

Franchising can mean taking on a big deal like running a shop for the Body Shop or McDonald's Restaurants or Kall-Kwik Printing, or it can mean providing a service on a small scale, using a business idea worked out by someone else.

There are now hundreds of franchised businesses to choose from. They can be single-person franchises such as window cleaning, domestic cleaning, colour counselling, image consulting, financial advice, drain clearing, driving instruction, kitchen fitting, legal advice on making wills, private car hire and chauffering, and many more. Or they can be larger businesses like dry cleaners, hairdressers, fashion shops, photo developers, pizza restaurants, office cleaning services, delicatessens or golf courses.

The range is very wide and you don't have to have knowledge of a particular type of business before you explore the possibility of taking on a franchise. You may have skills that are relevant from previous employment, but, in fact, many franchisors don't want people with direct experience of the same business because they prefer to teach their own particular method of doing business to people uncluttered by prior knowledge.

For and against franchising

For   Ready-made business idea
Tried-and-tested business concept and method
Easier to get loans from banks and other backers than
with an untried idea
Training provided

Against Needs money up-front, starting from £5000
Some income has to be paid long term to the franchisor
Little or no scope for personal innovation or input
Not suitable for creative people who need to do their
own thing

Points to watch

- Is your prospective franchisor a member of the British Franchise Association or other reputable trade body? If not, why not?
- Is the idea from abroad – and, if so, will it work in the British market?
- Is there a full manual on running the business for each franchisee?
- Is there training provided – and, if so, how adequate is it?
- Will there be further training?
- What competition will you face?
- What is the contract between the franchisor and other franchisees?
- Will the franchisor allow you to question existing franchisees – and, if not, why not?
- How realistic are the marketing, sales and research forecasts?
- Are the franchisor's last full years accounts available; if not, is this suspicious?

Ask for bank references and take them up. Get professional advice from banks, solicitors and accountants specialising in franchising, and don't be rushed into anything.

Information on franchising

Your local library or bookshop should have some books on franchising; there are also franchise exhibitions open to the public every year in London, Birmingham and Glasgow. The British Franchise Association can give you dates and details.

See the booklist at the end of this book for books on franchising; the address of the British Franchise Association is in Checklist 4.

Network marketing

Network marketing can be very profitable in a short time, but only if you know exactly what you are doing and how much time you want to commit to it. There are spectacular failures as well as spectacular successes in this type of business venture, which often attracts people with little or no business experience.

Avon, Tupperware and Betterware are some of the well-known names in this field and, more recently, the possibilities of making money out of selling costume jewellery have caught the public imagination as Cabouchon has recruited hundreds of women to sell jewellery to their friends and acquaintances, and the founder has become a millionaire.

Network marketing is also known as multi-level marketing or MLM. It's a method of selling goods or services direct to customers through a network of distributors who are constantly recruiting other distributors. A company using MLM recruits a network of independent distributors and they recruit others, forming their own networks. Products sold in this way vary widely, and range from financial and insurance services to lingerie, make-up, jewellery, household and kitchen equipment, and security products.

This type of business system had a bad reputation in the 1970s when pyramid selling systems requiring large entry fees and high fees for stock made profits difficult. These often extortionate payments were combined with impossible targets for the recruitment of other sellers and so many people suffered heavy losses. In addition, there were no refunds if you decided you had to pull out and stop trading. Bad publicity was widespread.

Nowadays, there are pyramid selling regulations which restrict entry fees to schemes to a maximum of £75 and many entry fees are now only about £25. If you decide to stop the business you can return the goods to the promoter and obtain a refund of 90 per cent, so the financial risks are reduced and much less one-sided than they used to be.

To succeed in the network selling you must be well-organised, self-motivated and, above all, you must really like selling. You may have to organise parties in your own and your friends' houses to sell your products. You will constantly be selling directly to the public, and that can include your friends, relatives and acquaintances, so you can't do it if you're the kind of person who gets embarrassed talking about money or your work, and likes to keep work and private life in separate compartments.

For and against network marketing

For Ready-made business idea
Training provided
Can work from home
Can be second income or full-time employment
Can grow rapidly

Against Need money up-front for entry to scheme and for stock
May not be a tried-and-tested idea
Can suffer from supply problems if product is new
May be over-hyped and over-priced

Points to watch

- Is your prospective network selling company a member of the Direct Selling Association? If not, why not?
- Does the company promoting the product or service have a good reputation?
- Does the concept already work in the British market? If it is a new company, how good is the administration, training and back-up for distributors?
- Are there product or service guarantees?
- Is there a full starter pack for each distributor on running your network marketing business?

- Is there training provided – and, if so, how adequate is it?
- Will there be further training?
- What is the contact between the distributor and the promoter company?
- Will the company allow you to question existing distributors – and, if not, why not?
- Do you really like the product and would you use it yourself?

Information on network marketing

It is important to know what you are letting yourself in for and strongly advisable to read a book about network marketing of MLM before committing yourself. See the booklist at the end of this book. See also Checklist 4 for addresses of organisations dealing with network marketing and direct selling.

Buying your own business

Taking the plunge and going into business for yourself for the first time by buying an existing business might sound like a good idea with no real drawbacks. But, like every business decision, it needs weighing up carefully before jumping on to the ice floe and taking your chances bobbing about in cold waters which others are no longer willing or able to bob about in.

10 vital questions to ask yourself

1. Why is the business for sale?
2. Do you believe the publicly given reasons for the sale?
3. Is this business really a going concern or are there hidden snags?
4. If you buy, will you have to accept restrictions on your trade for a certain length of time?
5. Does it have assets you can sell?
6. Does it have hidden debts or structural problems?
7. What are your motives for buying?
8. What is your assessment of the risks involved in buying the business?

9. Do you have a business plan and ideas of your own for the business?
10. Where do you see this business in five years' time?

PROTECTING YOUR BUSINESS

Intellectual property

This is the general term used to refer to laws intended to protect innovations and new ideas. These include patents, copyright, registered designs, unregistered design rights, trade and service marks, and confidential business information.

All businesses have confidential information – whether it's addresses of customers, a new marketing strategy and price lists or secret new designs for a manned rocket to the moon. You can ask people you employ to sign confidentiality agreements, as well as reminding them that they are trusted not to speak to competitors or to reveal certain information to anyone at all.

If you use freelances or outside contractors, you can ask them to sign agreements too. But, ultimately, you should be very careful with your confidential information because proving that a particular employee or business contact is the source of a breakdown in confidentiality is very difficult in law and it's much better to take steps to limit any possible damage in the first place.

Have locks on filing cabinets and offices, confidential codes for computer access and operate on a need-to-know basis, so that as few people as possible discover your highly sensitive information. This is usually going to be more secure than telling a number of people and expecting them all to keep to confidentiality agreements – and then when the damage is done, trying to work out whose fault it is.

Patents

These are the most legally powerful of all intellectual property rights and are intended to provide a monopoly right. The Patent Office receives more than 30,000 applications for patents per year, and its officials are keen to point out that a very wide variety of machines, products and processes (and the individual parts of them) across the whole spectrum of industry are patentable.

There are three basic criteria for a patent – whatever you are submitting must be new, inventive and capable of industrial application. But you must not disclose your new invention or design to anyone who is not under an obligation to keep it confidential, or you may be barred from getting a patent. It isn't simple and patenting your design can be a lengthy business. You would be well advised to get specialised help from a patent agent. For advice on patents, contact the Patent Office and the Chartered Institute of Patent Agents.

Copyright

This gives you rights as a creator of something like a painting, writing, music, photography, videotape, broadcasts, computer programs etc. There is no registration system of copyright in the UK. Your copyright is granted automatically, but if you do work for someone else, you may find that a contract is sent which assigns your copyright either totally or partially (i.e. worldwide or for use in one country – for ever or for one year – there are numerous variations) to the organisation which has commissioned you.

If you have a dispute, this is another complicated area where you should seek legal advice. Advice is available from different sources. For instance, the Writers Guild, the National Union of Journalists, the Independent Programme Producers Association (television programmes), the Institute of Practitioners in Advertising, the Performing Rights Society (musicians and composers), the British Copyright Council and other specialist trade or professional organisations, can all advise on copyright in their particular fields. See Checklist 2 at the back of this book.

Designs

These can be protected either by a registered design, which requires application to the Patent Office, or by design right which is unregistered and gives weaker but automatic protection without the need for registration.

Trademarks

Trademarks and service marks act as identification symbols used in the course of trade to enable the public to distinguish one trader's goods from the similar goods of other traders. Trademarks apply to goods and service marks apply to services. Not all trade and service marks are registrable.

If you have any doubts about your rights in the above areas, all of which can be complex, you should get advice from a patent agent, trademark agent or solicitor specialising in this area. For advice and information on all the above intellectual property issues, contact the Patent Office (address in Checklist 4 at the end of this book).

4

Getting Going – Planning and Finance

—■—

'If everybody minded their own business', the Duchess said in a hoarse growl, 'the world would go round a deal faster than it does.'

Alice in Wonderland, by Lewis Carroll

GETTING STARTED

Small business categories and terms

Before you set up any business, you need to know the different terms used to describe people who work for themselves. They sometimes overlap, but are not entirely interchangeable in meaning, so here are some definitions.

Self-employed

- Self-employed people are responsible for generating all their own income and paying their own business bills. They are not employed full-time by anyone.
- Commonly used to describe plumbers, electricians, builders, painters and decorators, and other trades.

- Other terms for the self-employed include jobbing, as in builder and gardener; temp or temporary, as in secretary; casual, as in labourer; and consultant, as in management or career.

Freelance

- A freelance is self-employed as a one-person business, using his or her own name, or a business name, but who works for other people – selling his/her own services by the hour, the day, the week, the month or per project.
- Commonly used to describe self-employed journalists, writers, editors, photographers, musicians, designers, technicians, computer programmers, television directors and midwives, among others.
- The term comes from the Middle Ages, when soldiers offered their lances, not free of charge but free of allegiance to any lord, and therefore outside the established feudal system where everyone had a place by swearing their loyalty to a nobleman. Freelances are still outside the established system, without allegiance to a single employer, so the term is still apt for its modern uses – even though it came into use 600 years ago and most freelances nowadays don't spend their time riding horses!

Small business person

- Describes a person running a small business, which may be a business partnership or limited company. Unlike freelances, these people are not selling their individual services alone, but those of the partnership or company.
- A person running a limited company has to be employed by the company and pay tax on tax Schedule E, which is called PAYE (pay as you earn), unlike the self-employed, who will mostly be on tax Schedule D, where payments are made in full, and tax is calculated and deducted later.

Consultant

Many people call themselves consultants. During the recession any executive made redundant could salve their bruised ego by saying they were 'doing some consultancy work' while waiting for a full-time job to come up.

The term used to be more exclusive and reserved for management consultants advising large corporations or senior hospital doctors. What all these people have in common is that they charge more for doing their work than someone who is not billed as a consultant. The idea is that the client is not just getting a few days' work, but a few days' work plus years of valuable experience and judgement. What all consultants *should* have in common is experience and expertise which they can sell to others through giving an overview as an outsider of a problem or project. A consultant can be a one-person business, or a consultancy can be run as a partnership or a company.

Using Consultants

Consultants don't always have a good name. Some people who aren't offering value for money, either in time or depth of expertise offered, have given a time-wasting image to the concept of 'consultancy'. Certainly 'working on a consultancy basis' has come to mean, in many people's eyes, 'you can expect to pay a lot for this'.

Judy Wagner, Managing Director of Finlayson, Wagner, Black – an executive recruitment consultancy based in Edinburgh – advises everyone to be careful when choosing consultants: 'There are so many people nowadays who call themselves consultants, but some of them are basically just doing little projects. Consultant used to mean something, but now anyone can call themselves a consultant. Redundant executives call themselves consultants while they're looking for a "proper" job.'

But all this doesn't mean that consultants are always a bad idea. They can be very useful to both small and large businesses because, provided they are chosen carefully, they can save a lot of time, effort and money by cutting through your business knots, blocks and problems with a valuable and experienced outsider's eye.

Consultants are there to stop you having to reinvent the wheel to solve a knotty problem. They should have expertise *you* can use to solve *your* problems.

For instance, you may want to expand your business but have no idea of how to put this into practice. You may find that your local Training and Enterprise Council has a deal offering you the services of a firm of management consultants at half price. You may decide you'd rather pay full price for a management consultancy recommended by a friend. Whatever the deal you settle on, you should know exactly what questions you are setting the consultant or consultants who are working with you and expect clear answers to the options you put to them.

To ensure this happy outcome, you need to write a brief setting out the problem or task you want them to work on. When you have written a brief you can go about choosing a consultant to work with you on it.

Writing a brief for a consultant

Describe the problem or task to be tackled.

- What do you expect the consultants to do? State the objectives clearly.
- What kind of action do you expect to take as a result of their work? Give clear information about your business.
- What resources can you offer from the business including staff time, desk space, phone line/s etc. to work with the consultants?
- What budget are you offering for the consultancy?
- What is the timescale? How long will the consultancy work take and when do you expect a final report?
- How do you expect the consultants to report conclusions to you?

Common mistakes when using consultants

- Expecting miracles.
- Expecting miracles fast.
- Expecting consultants to work without talking to both you and your staff.
- Not explaining the business fully.
- Not following the following guidelines.

Guidelines for choosing and working with consultants

- Are they recommended by anyone you know?
- If not, will they let you ring anyone on their client list?
- Do they have membership of any professional organisations?
- What relevant qualifications do they have?
- Have you seen their brochure?
- What is the basis for their fees?
- Will any of the work be subcontracted?
- What about confidentiality?
- Are there any conflicts of interest? (For instance, who owns the report or any subsequent development of software, training packages etc?)

Choosing between different consultancies

If you discuss your brief with different consultants, it must be on a confidential basis. Do any of them appear not to address some of the issues? Does this mean they don't have the relevant expertise? Do you trust them?

Evaluating the final report

These are the most important questions:

- Do you understand the recommendations?
- Do you accept the basis on which they are made?
- Are they practical?
- Have they solved your problem?
- Do you trust their judgement?

If yes – fine, pay up and get on with implementing the recommendations. **If not** – is it because your brief wasn't clear in the first place? Have you added on extra tasks but not extra time? Or is it because they haven't done their job thoroughly?

If you're not happy, negotiate. But be realistic – you can't suddenly ask a marketing consultant to include a detailed world sales survey of your product or service when you originally asked only for a sales survey of the UK and your place in that market.

If you really want more, you'll have to pay for it. You'll also have to work out whether you have the budget to pay for more consultancy.

Portfolio career person

A term invented by management guru Professor Sir Charles Handy to describe people who have a number of regular jobs and/or freelance commitments, making up a portfolio of work for different outlets.

Satisfying the tax inspector

Most people think it should be easy to decide whether you're employed full-time or part-time, or whether you're freelance and self-employed. And, in many cases, this is indeed very simple to define: anyone who has a full-time or part-time job working for someone else, and is being paid by them weekly or monthly, is employed. By contrast, anyone who runs their own business as a sole trader, and makes their own money, is self-employed.

The Inland Revenue says that you are self-employed if:

- you have the final say in how your own business is run;
- you are risking your own money in the business;
- you are responsible for meeting losses as well as profits;
- you hire other people and pay them yourself;
- you provide the equipment to enable you or others to do the job;
- you have to correct unsatisfactory work in your own time and at your own expense.

But what about situations where you are paid for freelance services while working in someone else's office, workshop, school or college, or on someone else's building site? Well, even if you are only employed for one day at a time, the tax inspector can argue that you are employed for that period, and that tax and National Insurance should be deducted by the employer before you are paid.

The Inland Revenue says that in this case you are in a 'master/servant' relationship, and therefore you are not self-employed when undertaking this work. So you will get a payslip with full tax and National Insurance deducted, even though you *wish* to be paid as a self-employed person, you *are* genuinely a self-employed person and you have no employment rights or benefits with that employer. Building workers can get tax exemption certificates under certain circumstances.

As a result, if, say, you are a freelance secretary who works part-time in someone else's office as well as offering secretarial services from your own home, you may find yourself being taxed both as a member of staff and as a freelance, even though you may think you are totally freelance. For you don't have to be taxed only one way – the tax system is not either/or. You may also pay National Insurance contributions twice – as an employee and as a self-employed person.

This issue is a very definite bone of contention between self-employed people and the tax authorities, and it makes a lot of work for accountants who are trying to get 'master/servant' decisions overturned. They also have to sort out the different sources of income and balance the tax already paid and the tax due for each tax year.

Self-assessment – Important Tax Changes

This is a new system of taxation for the self-employed and anyone setting up business now needs to find out about it. The big change is that profits for freelances and the self-employed – both sole traders and partnerships – are liable for tax much sooner than in the past. Instead of being taxed on your profits after you have completed each year of trading, profits are now taxed in the year they are earned. Hitherto, self-employed people did not have to pay any tax until at least 14 months after starting up.

Existing sole traders and partnerships stay on this system until April 1997. They move on to the new system sooner if there are changes in the ownership of the business, for instance if a partner retires or a new one joins. However, for all new businesses the new rules already apply. This is a big change for the self-employed and you need to take it into consideration when starting up and budgeting for your first year. Check what this means for you with your accountant and read CHECKLIST 1 – Income Tax, National Insurance and VAT – at the end of this book.

Seven steps to start creating your own work

1. **Work on your idea.** Read this book and others relevant to what you want to do – use your local library. Get advice from people you can trust and draw up a business plan.
2. **Open a bank account.** The first and most elementary step for a new freelance is a separate bank account for your business.
3. **Get an accountant.** Find an accountant who is reliable and inexpensive – ask other freelances for their advice. Your accountant will advise you of the best way to keep your day-to-day accounts.
4. **Deal with income tax.** Get information on income tax for the self-employed from your local tax enquiry centre.
5. **Sort out your National Insurance.** Get information on National Insurance for the self-employed – or the employed if you plan to be paid by your own limited company – from your local Social Security office.
6. **Think about value added tax (VAT).** Get information about VAT from your local Customs and Excise office.
7. **Corporation tax.** This step is for limited companies only: if you make profits in excess of salaries you may have to pay corporation tax on your profits. Ask your accountant for details.

See Checklists 1 and 4 at the back of this book for phone numbers to ring about income tax, VAT and National Insurance.

DECIDING ON YOUR BUSINESS NAME

The only small business options where you don't have to decide your business name are franchising and network marketing, because the name is part of the package you buy and you have to go with it as part of the deal.

If you buy an existing business, you may choose to keep the company name or you may decide to change it. If you set up your own business, whatever legal shape you choose you'll have to buckle down and decide on a name. This is a process which some people find hard and others think of as relatively easy. Whichever it is for you, you must take it very seriously.

What's in a name?

Names matter – they are part of the image and the wrong name for a celebrity or a business can be a handicap, just as the right name can be a springboard for success. When James Mason meets Judy Garland in the classic film *A Star is Born*, her character is called Esther Blodgett. Hearing this, he says: 'You must have been born with that name. You couldn't have made it up.'

The opposite reaction is true for trend adviser and forecaster Faith Popcorn. Anyone hearing her name thinks it must be invented. She's been spotting and forecasting social trends for 20 years, and claims that her clients who put money on her predictions in the 1980s about, for instance, increasing demands for fresh foods, for Mexican foods, for home delivery of goods and foods, a rising birthrate, the success of four-wheel-drive vehicles and the failure of New Coke, have been able to turn these interpretations of consumer trends into successful services, products and profits.

But that name? Is it for real? Is anybody really called Popcorn? No, it isn't. And they aren't. Faith Plotkin became Faith Popcorn because her first boss used to tease her about her surname, and call her variations such as Potkin, Papkin and Popkon, finally arriving at Popcorn and sticking with it as a nickname. She liked it so much she changed her name legally and even has Popcorn on her passport. It's an upbeat, light-hearted name, a talking point that provokes interest, and it suits her own image as someone in touch with trends and future developments.

Business names do's and don'ts

A business name should be useful, relevant, easy to remember and easy to find in the phone book. Does your business name fit these criteria? It should not be too jokey, as names that seem funny one year may seem very dated the next.

'If you see a bandwagon, it's too late,' says Sir James Goldsmith, former international businessman, who now concentrates on green politics. In short, your business name, as well as the names and slogans for your products and services, must be current (and that includes a deliberately old-fashioned name aimed at giving a new company immediate status – there are fashions and trends even in old-fashioned names) and not too complicated: The West End Garden Centre is a lot easier to remember than Mc-Clintock's West End Garden Equipment and Garden Innovations Centre.

The name must also be easy to say on the telephone. The Red and Yellow Lorry Company Limited would wear your tongue out in an hour! No wonder British Petroleum, taking advantage of the fashion for big companies to go for initials, became BP.

Business name checklist

Write down several names and play around with them – try these questions.

- Is it clearly relevant to you personally, or to your product or service?
- Is it easy to remember?
- Is there any other company or business with this name?
- Is it legal?
- Are you comfortable with it?
- Can you hear yourself saying this name every day?
- Do you believe in it?

Finally, once you decide on a name, make sure you put it in the phone book.

Business names and the law

Apart from the issue of credibility, there is also the issue of legality. There are two main areas of legislation on business names – the Business Names Act 1985 and the Companies Act 1989.

The Business Names Act

The Business Names Act 1985 applies to a company that trades under a name which is not its registered corporate name, and also to some sole traders and partnerships. If you are a sole trader using a business name other than your own surname, with or without your first names or initials, or if you are in a partnership which does not trade under the names of all the partners, you will have to comply with the Business Names Act.

If you are not registered as a limited company, you do not have to register your business name with anybody. If you trade under your own name – for instance as Annabelle Smith – you do not need to meet disclosure regulations, but if you trade as Annabelle Smith Marketing Services, you are classed as trading under a name which is not your own and you are required to display information at the place where you work – even if you work in a garage, in your garden, or in your spare room. This information must also be on all your business letterheads, receipts, invoices and all your business paperwork. It's a safeguard for both you and your customers, and suppliers, and is intended to guard against both dishonesty and the black economy.

You don't have to print everything. Plenty of small businesses use a specially made stamp and a printer's inked pad to stamp their business details on paperwork.

Example 1   Sole trader
This means, for instance, that a sole trader, John Smith, could trade as Smith, John Smith or J. Smith, but if he wanted to trade as J. Smith Plumber or John Smith Consultancy, the disclosure requirements would apply to him.

Example 2   Partnership
Similarly, a partnership consisting of Smith, Jones, Fry and Laurie would not be affected if they were trading as Smith, Jones, Fry and Laurie, but if they traded as Smith and Partners (or any other business name not including all the names of the partners), the disclosure requirements would apply.

Example 3   Company
A company using a trading name other than its own is also

affected by the disclosure rules. For instance, a company registered as 'XYZ Toys (UK) Limited', which was trading as 'XYZ Toys', would have to comply with disclosure regulations.

In practice, this means you need to include your business name, your own name and the names of any partners, directors or proprietors, plus your permanent business address.

For information on disclosure, contact the Department of Trade and Industry, Guidance Notes Section, Comanies Registration Office. For further information, contact Companies House and ask for their free leaflet on 'Business Names and Business Ownership'. See Checklist 4 at the back of this book.

The Companies Act

Company names are more strictly controlled than partnerships. There are regulations about company names and some names are not allowed to be used without permission from government or trade bodies.

Do's

- **Do** research existing names.
- **Do** consult Companies House, which has an Index of Company Names.
- **Do** consult the Trademarks Registry to check you are not trying to register a name the same as a trademark. The Registrar of Companies checks the companies register but not the Trade Marks Index.
- **Do** consult the Office of Fair Trading if you need to register under the Consumer Credit Act.

Problems can arise even if your name is accepted and registered. Another company with a similar name or trademark can officially object to your company name as being 'too like' their name and can lodge a complaint. If this is upheld, you can be directed to change your name, which can be both time consuming, costly and bad for business.

It is therefore sensible to get advice from a solicitor, or a company registration agent, before deciding to register the name for your company.

Don'ts

- **Don't** choose a name which is the same as another name already registered.
- **Don't** choose a name which is very similar to another name already registered.
- **Don't** choose a name which misleads the public – for instance, if you set up a general shop and call it 'Harrods', you may be liable to legal action for 'passing off' your business as being linked with a famous name.
- **Don't** choose a name that includes the words 'Limited', 'Unlimited' or 'Public Limited Company' or any abbreviation of these words, except at the end of the name to show the company's legal status.
- **Don't** use a name which gives the impression your company is connected with the government or a local authority, without getting approval.
- **Don't** use any of the names which need approval from the Secretary of State for Trade and Industry without getting permission.

It is sensible to consult a solicitor before choosing a business name. If your name is not legal in any way, it could cost you a lot of time, money and business goodwill to change it.

YOUR BUSINESS PLAN

WHENEVER you mention to other people that you're planning to go it alone, someone will utter the apparently daunting technical term 'business plan'. To many people who are setting out to keep their own accounts, and work out their own expenses and cash flow for the first time in their lives, it sounds frighteningly detailed, absolute and mathematically demanding. In fact, many people give up at this point and decide not to make the effort; they either abandon the idea of setting up on their own or decide to go ahead and muddle through anyway. Each of these responses has big drawbacks.

If you give up, you may be missing the chance of a lifetime to organise your life as you want it, and to use your talents and abilities in your own business. If you can spot a chance and work out what to do about it, you'll be progressing your own career, not sitting on your hands with a permanent nagging feeling that you may have missed something.

The poet T.S. Eliot put the whole thing very succinctly in a poem about a civil servant lamenting the boredom of his life and his missed opportunities.

> *For I have seen the moment of my greatness flicker*
> *And I have seen the eternal footman hold my coat, and snicker,*
> *And, in short, I was afraid.*

We all know there are times when we've missed opportunities in life, but this poem, called *The Love Song of J. Alfred Prufrock*, captures that sinking feeling when we realise we've missed out on something important and someone somewhere is definitely having a snide laugh at our expense.

Plunging in without a plan and muddling through may also produce laughter – in particular from the Inland Revenue when your incomplete accounts (no business plan and no accountant) finally make it on to their desk and they realise they've got a 'right one 'ere'!

Why you need a business plan

No business plan means no understanding of business expenses and what you can claim against tax. No plan means you may have missed an obvious business problem until it was staring you in the face and too large or too late to deal with. Actually, if you don't have any idea of the size, shape or structure of your own business, you may fail to spot several business problems and find that everything seems to go wrong at once.

But a business plan is not an exact object with an exact size and shape, and it does not stay the same for ever – it changes as your business changes. It is what *you* want it to be. And – even more important – what you *need* it to be. Just because a multinational company has a business plan the size of several paperback books, it doesn't mean yours has to be on the same scale. Your business plan is a tool for building your business, assessing your current position and potential, and setting out your ideas about your current and future markets.

Even if it's only two or three pages long, it's a vital asset, not only when you're getting started, but also as a constant detailed reference of background knowledge as you build up your business. You can start with one plan, then draw up another one after six months or a year.

A business plan is essential if you want to persuade people to lend you money. For example, if you want to borrow from a bank, or the government, or a local council, or the Prince's Youth Business Trust – which offers grants and loans to people aged 18 to 29 starting businesses – you must have a business plan. (See later in this chapter for more information on advice, training and finance from government, and from the Prince's Youth Business Trust.)

There is no magic formula and no great mystery about a business plan. It does not have to contain complicated sets of figures and graphs projecting sales, turnover, profits, running costs, marketing etc. for years to come.

What you *will* find, if you're prepared to spend a little time working out a basic plan that suits you, is that the time is very well spent, and will be useful time and again in the future. If you really can't get to grips with figures, fix an appointment with your accountant and thrash things out with him or her. If you haven't got an accountant, get one.

One in three new businesses fails within three years of starting up and, according to Barclays Bank, new businesses which start off with a plan are twice as likely to succeed as those which don't. It's logical, therefore, for Barclays and the other major banks to insist on seeing a business plan before they will consider making a loan to a new small business.

How to draw up your business plan

All the high street banks offer various kinds of small business starter packs, with forms setting out questions covering all the major areas of a basic plan. National Westminster claims to be the largest supporter of small business start-ups, with one in three of all new businesses and 1000 Small Business Advisers throughout the UK.

But whether or not you're going to ask a bank for help, the main points to cover in a business plan are fairly obvious.

General headings and guidelines

A general description of the proposed business.

- First state the name of the business and the type of business you're aiming at, and give a brief summary of your business idea.
- State what the legal identity will be, i.e. sole trader, partnership, limited company or co-operative.
- Estimate the number of people you will need, whether freelances, employees or partners, both when starting up and after a year's trading.
- List your major competitors and explain how your business differs from theirs – and why you think there is a gap in the market for your business.
- Outline your own relevant experience and qualifications.

The finance needed to get started.

- How much money do you need to get started?
- Do you have the money or do you need a loan?
- If you need a loan, do you want to borrow from a bank, from relatives or from another business person? Will you have a written agreement.
- Estimate how much you wish to borrow from a bank. State for how long you will need it, how you will pay it back and over what period.
- State what you wish to spend your loan on.

The market.

- Estimate your sales for each month of the first year and in total for the second year.
- Outline how you will reach your customers, e.g. advertising, direct sales, mail shots, cold calling etc.

The projected turnover.

- Give estimates of your projected costs and overheads during the first year. Then assess these against projected sales figures and give projected profits for the first year.
- Estimate when you expect your business to be in profit.

Your existing finance.

- Add up all your existing monthly payments.
- Give details of all the capital you require and how it will be repaid.
- List what security will be available if your business fails, e.g. your home.

This last point is vitally important to take note of. Most lenders expect at least half of the working capital for a new business to come from the business person themselves, and most people have only their home to use as collateral (a guarantee against loss) to pay off the borrowed half if things go wrong.

Whether you borrow from the banks or not, you could be putting your home at risk if you get deep into debt, as it may be your only available asset for paying off creditors.

However, if you don't have a business plan of any kind, you are taking much more of a risk than if you do. And many people who have drawn up plans for the first time have found them so helpful in sorting out their ideas that they refer to them and update them frequently.

Sample business plan

This plan is an outline intended to help you see the sort of information you need to plan your business or to persuade someone else to invest in your ideas. It is not a rigid strait jacket and, where it does not apply to your business, you should adapt it to suit you.

SECTION 1   YOUR BUSINESS

YOUR NAME

YOUR BUSINESS NAME – IF DIFFERENT

YOUR BUSINESS ADDRESS

DESCRIPTION OF YOUR BUSINESS

DATE YOU STARTED TRADING

DATE BUSINESS SET UP – IF APPLICABLE, e.g. TO PARTNERSHIP OR COMPANY

AIMS OF YOUR BUSINESS

IF SOLE TRADER – STATE HERE

IF PARTNERSHIP – LIST PARTNERS – LIST CAPITAL INVESTED AND PERCENTAGE OF OWNERSHIP

IF LIMITED COMPANY – LIST SHAREHOLDERS WITH NUMBER OF THEIR SHARES AND PERCENTAGE OF TOTAL

SECTION 2   LIST YOUR STAFF – PART-TIME OR FULL-TIME – IF APPLICABLE

NAME●AGE●POSITION●DATE OF JOINING● SALARY/WAGES

QUALIFICATIONS
TOTAL OF EMPLOYEES – INCLUDING PARTNERS OR DIRECTORS

SECTION 3   YOUR PRODUCT OR SERVICE

1. Outline briefly the products or services you are offering or intend to offer with the prices charged

2. Outline the market you are entering – its size and history over the past ten years if possible.

List your actual and potential customers

Assess your market in terms of whether it is growing or shrinking

3. List your major competitors with their strengths and weaknesses

4. Your expected turnover in your first year   £

Your sales break even figure   £

Your reasons for believing you can reach your expected first year turnover

5. Describe any market research you have done – if applicable

Describe your marketing and sales plans

6. List your major suppliers

List any alternative suppliers

Explain why you buy from these suppliers and what advantages they offer you

SECTION 4   YOUR BUSINESS PREMISES

(Include what is applicable to you from this list – for instance, if you are working from home, state this, and state the value of your home and any mortgage you have or rent you pay)

1. Describe your place of work, e.g. office/workshop/both

2. Freehold or leasehold?

3. What is the market value of your place of work?

4. Give details of mortgage or rent, e.g. the total amount of any mortgage you have taken out with monthly repayments
OR list the rent you pay per year, the length of the lease and date of next rent review

5. State the rates you pay – total per year
– method of payment (monthly/quarterly/annual)

6. State who is responsible for repairs to your place of work

SECTION 5   YOUR BUSINESS EQUIPMENT

1. Describe the equipment you use

Date when replacement needed

Current value

Describe any hired equipment/or equipment bought on loan –

list payments –

list length of loan

2. List equipment needed in the next 12 months, the cost – and how you intend to pay for it

SECTION 6   YOUR ASSETS AS SECURITY

1. List your business assets with their value, e.g. equipment

2. List your personal assets with their value

SECTION 7   THE FINANCE YOU NEED

1. List the amount of money you need to start the business and/or a loan for a specified time to help you expand

List equipment you need to buy with costs

List equipment total

List other start-up or expansion expenses, e.g. rent in advance

List expenses total

List your own money invested or to be invested and/or partners and shareholders

List any grants, e.g. government, European, private, Princes Youth Business Trust etc.

List total loan required – if applicable

If you have already started trading, give details of your monthly accounts for the past year plus a projected budget for the next two years.

If you are not yet trading, supply a projected cash flow for the next two years. This may sound formidable to those unused to business. But it can be simplified to include your projected monthly income and total turnover, and all your outgoings, including for example equipment costs, supplies, rent, rates, phone, electricity, fees to accountant/book keeper, staff (if applicable), loan repayments, advertising, travel, car/van, stationery etc.

Finally, put yourself in the position of the person you want to lend you money or invest in you and your business.

Read your plan. Have you presented a convincing and accurate picture of what you plan to do? Is there anything you've forgotten? Are there any holes in your research? If so, plug them now. Your business plan can be a great asset and can be the difference between a successful income for you and muddling through from hand to mouth. Take time over it and you should find you have a much clearer view of what you're doing, and why and how.

Business plans – common mistakes

- Building on dreams without pinning them down to realities. Stick to the facts. If you build in inaccurate forecasts you're likely to end up in debt. Your business plan must be realistic.
- Taking your current sources of income for granted.
  Always ask yourself – what's the current real strength of the income I get from each source? How long will this source of income last? What new income could I replace it with? What plans do I have for getting new income?
- Being too rigid in applying the plan. Your business plan is not a rigid framework set in concrete. It's not an answer to all your problems if you stick to it come what may, because what may happen, almost certainly will happen, is change. In the next three years there will be changes in your business and changes in your business environment. For example, you may rely on one contact for some of your income and when that individual leaves or that customer is taken over, suddenly you no longer have that work – either because it has disappeared or because someone else has been given the contract or the commission to do it. What do you do? Of course you set out to find other work and that other work may expand another already existing area of your employment or it may lead you to do something completely new. As a result of all this you will find your business plan no longer fits the shape of your business. Are you

still on target financially? If so change the plan – don't worry about changing a new and successful part of your turnover. Build on where you are, not where you think you should have been by now.

■ Not using your business plan. If you take the trouble to sort out a basic business plan, but then subsequently never look at it, are you being sensible or prudent? Everyone who is working for themselves and generating their own income every day is, of necessity, very busy and concerned with plenty of detail. If you never look at your business plan, you may think you remember the broad principles of the plan and the methods you're going to use to establish your goals, but you may be missing out because you forget vital pointers to your future which came out in the plan.

Ask all the questions – even the awkward ones

'It's so simple. Step one: you find the worst play in the world, a surefire flop. Step two: I raise a million bucks. There are a lot of little old ladies in the world. Step three: you go back to work on the books, only list the backers, one for the government and one for us. You can do it Bloom. You're a wizard. Step four: we open on Broadway, and before we can say step five, we close on Broadway. Step six: we take our million bucks, and we fly to Rio de Janeiro.'

This is Zero Mostel as Max Bialystock, the theatre impressario in Mel Brooks's film *The Producers*. But his plan to make money out of a bad musical called *Springtime for Hitler* does not work because he never asks 'What if the show is so bad it's a hit?'

3 hot tips!

1. Always ask yourself: What if . . . ? Even if contracts, deals, suppliers, customers or employees appear safe and secure, always have alternative plans.
2. Never assume – assumptions can kill your business.
3. Always investigate – questions can keep your business alive.

FUNDING

Not every business needs outside funding when it starts. You may need very little capital to get going, particularly if you are working from home. Or you may have capital of your own – possibly from savings, inheritance or a redundancy payment. But if you do need a loan or a grant to get you started, where do you go for money and how can you be sure you're getting a good deal?

In simple terms there are four main categories of funds for new businesses:

- family and friends;
- government schemes;
- banks;
- venture capital.

Family and friends

Many people rely on their family or friends for a loan to get started, or an investment in shares if their new business is a limited company. There are advantages and disadvantages to borrowing money in this way. What do you do if the money is suddenly required before the agreed term of the loan is over? 'But I need that money now to buy a new car – you've had your turn, now I want it back.' What about friendships or family relationships if you lose the loan? You could be putting a lot more at stake in your life than just money: 'How could you do that to your father/mother/uncle/sister/cousin/best friend?'

Poisoning family or friendly relationships with disputes over money is not an attractive prospect and, if you do go ahead on this path, you would be well advised to get an agreement properly drawn up by a solicitor so that everyone knows exactly where they stand and what they are letting themselves in for. Of course, not all family loans end in financial disaster, but if they do, things can only get even worse!

Government schemes

The Small Firms Loan Guarantee Scheme is run by the Department of Trade and Industry (DTI), and provides a government guarantee against default by borrowers by guaranteeing at least 70 per cent of loans ranging from £5000 to £100,000 to new and existing businesses. Between 1981 and 1993, more than £1 billion worth of loans to 33,000 firms were covered in this way.

The DTI also offers financial help for consultancy projects in companies employing fewer than 500 people, as well as regional investment grants, and other regional aid within Development Areas, Intermediate Areas and Inner City Areas; management advice; and information and grants for research projects.

Grants and loans from government-backed organisations can be found if you know where to look. For instance, the Sports Council, the Arts Council, the Crafts Council, the Rural Development Commission, and Training and Enterprise Councils may be able to help you if your planned business falls into categories for which they have training funds or financial help.

The Department of Employment also offers Career Development loans in partnership with Barclays, Co-operative and Clydesdale Bank. You can borrow between £200 and £8000 to pay for training or study. Repayments are at low rates of interest. See Checklist 4 for address.

Regional aid

You can also apply for help with finances or training for new businesses from regional agencies. Information about urban regeneration funds in England can be obtained from ten regional offices – the numbers are listed in Checklist 4 at the end of this book. These offices were set up in April 1994 to centralise more than 20 different schemes run by four different government departments – Employment, Environment, Transport, and Trade and Industry.

Contact the Scottish Office, the Welsh Office and in Northern Ireland the LEDU (Local Enterprise Development Unit) for information, advice and financial help to small local firms employing up to 50 people.

European help in your field

For information on European Community regulations, grants, loans, training schemes and new developments in the Community, you can contact the Department of Trade and Industry, which has a number of very useful booklets or the European Commission office in London.

The European Commission has an Information Point to deal with queries and can advise you where to start finding out answers to your questions. Their library is also open to the public – their address and phone number can be found in Checklist 4 at the back of this book.

Banks

The first thing to emphasise about banks is that they are there to make money out of you, and you need to choose your bank very carefully if you don't want them to do too well out of the deal. Banks may all look similar to an undiscerning eye, but they vary a lot in the type of services they offer, and the range and level of charges they make.

In the past banks have come in for a lot of criticism because they never published the charges they made to their hard-working customers, especially those on business accounts. Under the Code of Banking Practice, banks are now obliged to publish their tariffs for personal accounts and have also been pressured by customers into publishing their tariffs for business accounts.

However, you must read these tariffs very carefully and, if you don't understand exactly what is being charged for each service, it's a good idea to write and ask for an explanation in writing. The best advice is to be constantly vigilant and make time to check your statements every time they arrive. You'll have read in the papers about enormous and distressing mistakes in bank credits, debits and charges, so be warned and keep a sharp eye on your accounts, both business and personal.

Bank charges – points to check

Charges can vary for:

- the charge per number of cheques credited or debited;
- standing orders;
- stopping cheques;
- fees for bounced cheques;
- monthly maintenance fees;
- overdrafts;
- unauthorised borrowing (i.e. going into the red without an overdraft arrangement);
- special presentation of cheques;
- cheques in foreign currency.

Shop around. Find out exactly what banks offer small businesses. Remember that a few pence more per transaction adds up to a lot of pounds per year – for the bank not you.

Bank overdrafts and loans

What do banks look for in financial terms when you turn up to ask them for a loan or an overdraft to enable you to start or expand your business? And what is the difference between an overdraft and a loan?

A bank loan is a fixed amount of money borrowed for a fixed length of time, with a written agreement and repayments every month. If you fail to pay up, your business assets, and also your home, can be forfeited and sold by the bank to get their money back.

An overdraft is a borrowing arrangement which allows you to go into the red or in other words be overdrawn on your account temporarily if necessary. It's intended to meet the day-to-day needs of your business, whereas a loan is usually part of a long-term strategy.

However, every business is different and not everyone needs a loan or an overdraft. For instance, if you have a business where you don't have to buy in a lot of supplies or equipment to start trading, you may never need to borrow from the bank, unless you want to expand and you need money to do so. In addition, banks are now reporting that the problems many small businesses had during the recession at the beginning of the 1990's seem to have put some people off going to the banks for start-up money, preferring to use their own capital instead.

For their part, banks are now offering a range of services aimed at being user-friendly for new businesses, both when they start up and when they need capital to expand. The major banks have very useful practical booklets packed with ideas and information for people wanting to start a new business. They also have forms outlining how to structure a basic business plan, so you could find it useful to collect small business information from as many different banks as possible and compare what they have to offer. Remember, *you* can interview *them* – make them realise you know they are competing for your account!

How to get a bank loan

If you want a loan, bank staff always want to see your business plan – and they usually expect you to look like a person who can run his or her own business. Anita Roddick's story of how she and her plans for her first Body Shop were rejected when she wore T-shirt and jeans to the interview, but were accepted when she went back in a suit, still apply today. You may believe that you, too, can go on to conquer the business world wearing T-shirts and jeans – but, before you win your style victories, if you need the bank's money, you need to think about how you and your business look to the people who can lend you the money.

The bank will want to know that the business is well run by people of integrity who are not likely to push off to South America or the South Seas once they have their hands on the bank's gleaming shekels. Whether you are asking for a loan or an overdraft facility, the health of the balance sheet, your budgeting, cash flow forecasts, purchasing, pricing policy, marketing and the current state of your market are just a few of the issues you must be well prepared to discuss.

The Banking Ombudsman

If you have a serious problem with your bank – such as money being transferred without your permission from your personal account into your business account or the bank somehow managing to lose your cash takings which you put in the deposit machine – you may be able to complain to the Banking Ombudsman.

Since the scheme started in 1986, it has always been possible for personal customers, sole traders, partnerships and unincorporated companies to take their complaints to the Banking Ombudsman. Limited companies were, however, excluded. But since January 1993 the scheme has been extended to cover limited companies with a turnover of up to £1 million a year.

Venture capital

Companies set up to provide capital available for investment in businesses that want to expand sound rather like a dream come true. For many small businesses, unfortunately, obtaining venture capital is often difficult and remains a dream.

Research by accountants Touche Ross has shown that fewer than 5 per cent of applications to companies offering venture capital are likely to succeed, and many small companies cannot get funds simply because the amounts they are seeking are too small for the specialists in this field who are looking to invest millions and make more millions. However, even if you do find someone willing to invest in your company, you have to recognise that you will usually have to give up part of your equity in exchange for an injection of funds. Shares, directorships – everything is negotiable.

In Germany, banks are allowed to invest venture capital in businesses, but in Britain this is not permitted, so National Westminster Bank has been trying to generate goodwill by compiling lists of so-called Business Angels which it can put in touch with businesses needing capital. Both Lloyds Bank and Barclays have staff who can provide assessments of companies with new technological developments.

You can get advice from Training and Enterprise Councils about possible sources of venture capital (for more information about TECs see later in this chapter). TECs may offer free or subsidised advice and advisers to help you find an investor, and make a deal, and they should be able to inform you about publications and organisations in the venture capital field.

Other capital for small businesses

The Prince's Youth Business Trust

For younger people wanting to get started in business, the Prince's Youth Business Trust (PYBT) can provide grants and loans to people under the age of 30 who are out of work, or members of ethnic minorities, disabled people, ex-offenders or people from deprived backgrounds. You must have a viable idea for starting up in business and be unable to obtain money from other sources (i.e. you must have been turned down by banks).

You will be given some business training and helped to produce a business plan, but you must show evidence of commitment and initiative. The founder and president of the scheme, which was set up in 1986 and is separate from the Prince's Trust, is Prince Charles, and the PYBT has so far helped nearly 20,000 young people starting up a wide variety of businesses. Surveys show a good record of success, with two-thirds still trading after three years, and a handful of young entrepreneurs already with turnovers of around £1 million.

Grants are up to £1500 to individuals and £3000 for groups of people wanting to start a business. Loans for stock, equipment or working capital are also available up to £5000 – averaging around £2000. No interest is charged in the first year, and interest rates are very low and well below market rates in the second and third years. Money for the trust is raised from the private sector and matched pound for pound by the government.

On-going advice, with each person who gets a grant getting a business adviser as well, has clearly contributed to the staying power of the new businesses funded by the PYBT. Prince Charles has described the success rate as 'a remarkable achievement when you consider that the PYBT is in the risk business. If we were merely to help those who could virtually guarantee success, there would be little point in the work. Those people could go elsewhere for their support. It is my intention that we should take a risk and help those who have the courage to take risks themselves. They are likely to be the sort of people we will hear about in the future. Among them are bound to be some who will rise to the top in industry or commerce. They show they have the necessary spirit, the necessary enthusiasm and enterprise to get to the top.'

The Prince's Youth Business Trust covers England, Wales and Northern Ireland, and the Prince's Scottish Youth Business Trust covers Scotland.

CASE HISTORY:

A Glass Act

Subject	Mark Prest
Current role	Sole trader, Mark Prest Glass
Nature of business	Produces an exclusive range of hand-painted enamelled glassware and a range of one-off unique kiln cast glass sculpture pieces, and sells to Liberty's and other outlets in London, as well as Ireland, the US and Canada
Location	Manchester Craft Centre
Hours worked	8–12 hours a day, 6 days a week – and sometimes Sundays to complete orders
Employees	Just Mark
Turnover	The first year was £2500, second year £10,000 and third year £15,000
Advertising/ marketing	Takes advantage of the opportunities that magazines offer: 'I do three or four trade shows a year, and all the journalists come round and interview you and use pictures of your work. I've been in several national magazines and that brings in business.' The Crafts Council do a lot of press releases and Mark has had publicity via them – for instance, he exhibited at the Chelsea Crafts Fair, the top show for contemporary craftspeople in

> Europe: 'I don't advertise – I have price lists
> and coloured postcards of my work. Brochures
> are difficult to justify because they cost
> hundreds of pounds to produce – and,
> hopefully, your work is constantly changing,
> so they soon get out of date'

MARK PREST worked part-time in supermarkets and a mail order
warehouse while taking his 'O' levels at college. But between the ages
of 18 and 20 he was unemployed, during which time he made up his
mind to go into landscape design: 'I'd always been interested in art
but didn't have the confidence in my talent,' he says.

He had done some ceramics, and took an 'A' level in sculpture in
order to be accepted to do a degree course: 'I only had a maintenance
grant, so I had to work part-time in a pub to pay my way through
college. Then I did my degree and still had to work in the pub.'

Mark did an Arts Foundation course at Stourbridge College and
left in 1989 not really knowing what to do next. 'I had no business
training during my course,' he says, 'and I couldn't train with
anyone because most people working with glass are one-person
studios.'

He considered taking a management course, but instead decided to
go on a three-month course called Graduate Enterprise Programme,
funded by the government for graduates who want to set up in
business. It covered basic business skills such as how to write a
business plan, marketing and how to get funding.

'It was very intensive and the whole goal of the course was to
produce a business plan,' says Mark. 'A high percentage of the people
on that course are still in business. It was very useful and people have
commented on the fact I seem to be more business aware than other
people with arts qualifications. I believe strongly that people on arts
courses must have business training.'

Despite his training, Mark's business plan to set up his own studio
was rejected by the first bank he approached. Then he went to the
Prince's Youth Business Trust, which helps young people turned
down by banks. 'I got a grant of £1000 and a loan of £2500, plus an
expansion loan of £1500 from the PYBT – and I had a £1000 overdraft
facility from another bank,' he says.

Mark started running his own business in 1991, a week before he
was 26, and now sells to Liberty as well as galleries and shops in
Germany, Ireland, the US and Canada. He's also sold to the Victoria
and Albert Museum and to a museum in Hull.

'I get the customers usually through trade shows or publicity in magazines,' he says. 'I work in a studio in a craft centre which is open to the public. There are silk painters, jewellery and fashion designers, and people making ceramics and other crafts. We lease the premises from the council, and everyone pays rent on a studio – it's cheaper than a retail outlet, but I have to pay business rates, rent, overheads etc. It's not subsidised and is run as co-operative with about 20 different businesses.'

Mark says he hasn't had a holiday in three years and that the most stressful thing is the financial side of the business: 'Banks are unsupportive, and the only thing they look at is figures; my business would have gone under if it hadn't been for me fighting to keep it going. If you run your own business you have to be a tough person, because if you don't have stamina you won't survive.'

Q. What mistakes did you make at the start?
A. The worst mistake I made was being undercapitalised: I didn't have any money of my own and I quickly got into money difficulties. In the first year, I was ignorant about trade fairs, so I didn't do any. I've done four trade shows this year – they are expensive but the more often you go, the more the buyers see you and believe in you.

Q. What are the best and the worst things about being self-employed?
A. The best thing is the freedom. I like going to the trade fairs and meeting other creative people. I go to exhibitions and trade fairs, and I met Prince Charles once. Art has a glamorous image, but I'm doing it because I want to, not for the surface glamour. People say 'Oh, Mark's landed on his feet', but you don't just land on your feet – you make it happen.

The worst things are pressure and money. Late payers are the biggest problem. Originally all my exports were pro forma, paying in advance; then this Canadian customer said they would pay within 30 days and in fact it's taken two months. They are a big customer so I can't hassle them, but the problem is I have to pay the rent whether the money's there or not. And if the money's not there, I have to pay charges at the bank. Some clients always pay promptly. But it is a problem and I think there should be a law enforcing payments.

Q. How do you see the future?
A. I think there is a future for small businesses: small businesses

create things that big businesses don't and I think it should be pushed as a career path for young people. But more support is needed from the government, including more government-run courses and a law on late payments.

Q. *What advice would you give to others?*
A. The first thing is to think about your business idea very carefully and make sure that it's what you really want to do. Then get as much advice as possible and produce a very good business plan, with details of what you're going to produce, the market, the premises etc. Be as prepared as you can be – and also be prepared to give things up and go without.

FINANCIAL ROUTINES

Routine can be the saviour of a small business – though we may not all want to follow the builder who worked every day from eight in the morning to three in the afternoon and then went home to do his accounts – every day. Spending an hour on his accounts, he argued, was worth more money than all the rest of the day's work, because, in his own words, 'Sitting down at my desk is when I really make money'. His point was that, by doing his accounts in detail every day without fail, he kept track of all his expenses, never lost a receipt or failed to send an invoice.

This technique, too rigorous for many, is the opposite extreme from those unfortunate small business people who say, 'I never bother with accounts – I just send an invoice when I run out of money'. I call them unfortunate because although they do burn the midnight oil less frequently than most of us while doing their accounts and they may *seem* happy, they are in fact always losing money and creating a lot of unnecessary stress for themselves as well.

I once received an invoice for work done by an electrician more than nine months after the work was completed. I'd forgotten all about this bill and I queried it because I assumed he'd been paid already. In fact, he hadn't. He was one of those who keep grubby, folded bits of paper in the back pockets of their jeans, then add these to a pile of other grubby bits of paper in a drawer or a shoebox and then forget about them until a nasty letter arrives from the bank manager.

My electrician's explanation was that he thought of these grubby, folded-up potential invoices as money in the bank, which he could call on when he needed them. To him, this totally insecure way of running his business finances was a form of security. He just didn't see that the reality was the complete opposite.

Other people pointed out to him that he frequently lost money as he could not always remember all the costs of a job or the agreed price – and, sometimes, as he cheerfully admitted, he even completely forgot to invoice a client or clients moved so they never got the chance to pay the bill. He also made it more difficult to get hold of the money he was owed and created more (unpaid) work for himself because, like me, many people assumed his invoices had already been paid and either ignored it as an error or refused to pay until he phoned them up (more unnecessary cost).

He could never grasp the concept that he could turn his hard work into money much earlier and use money he didn't need immediately to earn interest in the bank or building society. Neither did he understand that he was losing even more money by paying for an overdraft at the bank.

These two contrasting examples, of rigid routine on the one hand, and complete lack of any regular financial system on the other, are extremes of organisation and disorganisation. But many people have variations on the inefficient extreme, ranging from forgetting to keep account of business expenses – whether incurred on specific jobs, or losing track of general expenses incurred in running equipment, telephones or cars.

When you're working for yourself, lapses into inefficiency always cost you *your* money. If you don't manage your time well, *you'll* be the loser.

Most people will find that writing up very basic accounts every day in outline and then spending a minimum of an hour once a week in detail will keep them ahead of the game. This is followed by quarterly accounts if you're registered for VAT and annual accounts – usually worked out by an accountant – for the Inland Revenue. All this will keep you ticking over efficiently and cost-effectively.

Accountants

YOU MAY have heard the story of the three accountants who go for a job interview. The first one goes into the interview room and is asked 'What's two and two?' He gives the correct answer. So does the second accountant in her interview; she, too, knows her maths. The third accountant is then asked the same question. He pauses, looks thoughtful, then says: 'Two plus two? What would you like it to be?' He gets the job.

What accountants can do for you

You may not think of accountancy as a joking matter, but this little story offers an insight into the simple and unvarnished fact that accounts are not set in stone. Figures are not just figures. They are interpretations. Good accountants can be worth far more than their fees.

Systems for paperwork

'With any small business you don't just let things lie – you've got to keep things moving,' says Ted Bonner of E.G. Exports. 'When I get an enquiry, I like to get a quote back out again within two days. If I haven't done that I feel I've lost. You have to keep on top of paperwork and be strict about that.'

Book-keeping

Some people do this on paper, others want everything on computer screen. Some people want to do it all themselves, others prefer to get a book-keeper to come in once a week or once a month at the start (some people prefer to use an accountant for book-keeping, but a book-keeper costs less than an accountant).

You must decide for yourself how you're going to deal with the book-keeping. Ask other small business people – not your competitors – what they do. Then make a judgement in the light of your own business needs, both current and expected.

If you are a sole trader, and you have registered for VAT, you may find that keeping your quarterly VAT accounts gives you an accurate enough of an idea of your cash flow and the shape of your business. However, if your business is more complicated – especially if you are running a company – you may be well advised to have a book-keeping system run by a trained book-keeper.

How to find a book-keeper

'Ask your friends running small businesses if they know a good person. Word of mouth is usually a good way of finding someone reliable,' says Colin Murphy of The Bookkeeping Bureau. 'I would advise that all businesses, even very small businesses, should have a book-keeping system which is computerised and runs on a monthly basis. The world is different now. It'll never be like the 1980s when money was coming in all the time – you need to know exactly where you are financially. You can't afford to let things drift, whether you have a manual or computerised system. But I believe computerised is always better.'

Cash flow

'When you first start, cash flow is vital, but often a guess,' says Fiona Price, of Fiona Price and Partners Ltd. 'You must have good sound financial controls on the business and revisit your cash flow weekly. At the beginning, profit is a luxury whatever people tell you. Cash flow is the lifeblood. We look at cash flow every month and our projections are generally pretty accurate.'

Maintaining cash flow

Most banks have forms they can provide for you to fill in your cash flow forecasts. In simple terms, this means the income you expect to receive and the expenditure you expect to make. Forecasting income includes knowledge of money owed to your business and being able to predict reasonably accurately when that money will come in, so that you don't end up becoming insolvent because you've spent or agreed to spend money you haven't yet got.

If you can't get the money in to pay the rent or the telephone bill, you may have done a lot of work but still have to cease trading because the cash just isn't there to pay the bills. Sometimes companies go bust with money owing to them which in theory would be more than enough to pay off their debts to others. But because they couldn't collect that money, it remains unreal and therefore of no help to them.

OTHER HELP

Training for women, ethnic minorities and unemployed people

Free or cheap training may be available in your area for women, women returners and ethnic minorities. If you are unemployed, you may be eligible for free training to give you new skills or brush up your skills, with extra benefit paid while you are training. Start-up grants for small businesses are also available to the long-term unemployed.

Women returners are women with children who have dropped out of the world of work or who are working part-time at jobs below their skills and capacity. In other words, they are returning to the world of work after a career break and may need retraining before they re-enter the market place.

The Women Returners Network produces a directory each year of education and training for women, and there are some women returners' training and retraining courses available at Further Education colleges paid for or subsidised by the government, the European Community or Training and Enterprise Councils. Some women want to return to the workplace part-time when their children go to school, but when you set up your own business as a working mother you should be aware that part-time work may not always be a realistic option in some cases. Pick your work carefully.

I started up my first business because I was a mum with small children and I wanted to fit work in around the children. I think a lot of women think it would be nice to work part-time, but if you set up a business and it's successful, you can't control the hours. If you're really serious about your business, it takes over your life. You can't really do it part-time unless you're selling a skill or a service where you take on projects and know the work involved right at the start.

Angela McLean, Rainbow Cleaning Services

Help for disabled people

Many disabled people are able to run their own businesses from home or from a workplace outside the home.

Particular disabilities have organisations and associations offering specialised help and advice; there are also general organisations, such as the Disabled Living Foundation, which can advise on equipment, tools or aids you may need to help you work and will offer advice on applying to the Disablement Advisory Service which lends equipment etc. Applications can be made at your local JobCentre.

You can also apply at the JobCentre for help with travel costs incurred in getting to work and you may be eligible for government-funded training. Employers can get grants to help them adapt buildings – for instance, by installing a lift – to make it possible for them to employ a disabled person.

Whether your disability is lifelong or you are newly disabled, you can get information on all the above from your local JobCentre, and from RADAR, the Royal Association for Disability and Rehabilitation. Disabled people have legal rights to help with daily life both at home and at work, and RADAR has booklets outlining how you can get the most out of your working life. See Checklist 4 at the back of this book.

YOUR LEGAL OBLIGATIONS

Employers' liability

When you start up your own business, you may find yourself employing another person or persons for the first time. Apart from the skills of people management – which can be learnt, to some extent, from experience and by talking to friends who already employ people themselves – you do have some legal obligations.

The first and most pressing is that all employers must insure against liability for personal injury and disease sustained by their employees, and arising out of, or in the course of, their employment in Britain. The amount of insurance should be at least £2 million. It sounds a lot, but in most cases policies give unlimited cover. You need to ring up an insurance broker or insurance company and ask them to give you a quote for this. A copy of the employers' liability certificate must be displayed at the place of work at all times. All workers including casual workers are classed as employed under the Employers' Liability (Compulsory Insurance) Act 1969. You will not need to take out employers' liability insurance for domestic servants employed solely to work in a private househould, if you only employ relatives in your business, or if you contract work out to other freelances at their places of work.

Insurance

Insurance is a necessity if you set up a business in premises away from your home. If you are working at home, it is important to check your home insurance and update it in line with the value of equipment, fire risks etc. A separate policy for your business should be considered.

There often seems to be a bewildering amount of insurance around when you set up in business. Some people solve things by getting a standard package from an insurance adviser or their bank, offering cover for fire, special perils and theft, often for all risks and including loss of profits or business interruption and insurance against glass damage. Other types of cover include insurance against damage to goods in transit, against dishonest employees and for employees travelling on behalf of the business.

Here is a checklist of common insurance policies so you can decide which are most appropriate for you and your business, and discuss your needs with your insurance adviser. Not all insurance advisers are registered, but insurance brokers have to be registered under the Insurance Brokers Act 1977.

Insurance checklist

Buildings and contents insurance
Business all-risks insurance
Business interruption insurance
Directors and officers insurance
Household insurance
Legal expenses insurance
Liability insurance
Life insurance
Medical expenses insurance
Money insurance
Motor insurance
Permanent health insurance
Personal accident insurance

Employers' liability insurance
Engineering insurance
Fidelity insurance
Fire insurance
Goods in transit insurance
Plate glass insurance
Prize indemnity insurance
Products liability insurance
Professional indemnity insurance
Public liability insurance
Theft insurance
Traders' combined insurance
Travel insurance

Personal accident insurance

Anyone working for themselves should look at the range of policies available for personal accident insurance because, if you have an accident, you are likely to find that the tiny benefits available to the self-employed via the Department of Social Security are not enough to keep you from financial ruin. In addition, your business is very vulnerable while you are unable to function normally and the stress of this can hinder your recovery if you are not adequately insured.

Life insurance and pensions

Do you have any life assurance or a pension scheme of any kind? If you are your business, it is important to sort this out.

Working at home

Many insurers now provide home/office insurance policies specifically for people working from home and this will cover your work equipment, with costs varying according to the amount you need to insure. Some insurance companies offer cover for legal expenses as well and this can be vital if you have a dispute with a client who refuses to pay up on a large payment due to you.

Crisis planning – fire – burglary – flood

Whether your workspace is home or away, how would your business be affected if you had a fire/flood/burglary and lost your business records? Have you got back-up disks of work on your computer in a safe place? For instance a metal box or a fire-proof safe? These are available from office equipment shops. Do you store vital software away from your workspace? If you've never thought about any of this, think of it now and assess the risks you're taking. How long would it take you to recover if disaster struck? How much time and money would you lose?

Wills

If you, your partner or your business partner dies, whoever has to deal with the business implications of this may find there are financial problems they have never considered before. Problems which could handicap them in business simply because of the lack of a few simple steps.

No will?

Obvously, if you or your colleagues do not have a will, the problems of probate – proving that the estate (everything that belongs to a deceased person) is really legally theirs and able to be inherited at all – can take months longer than if a will exists. This kind of delay can freeze all a dead person's assets and they cannot be used by anyone, often for many months.

In addition, the estate of someone who dies intestate (the legal term for dying without a will) can be claimed against by all living close relatives, so a partner may have to sell a house or a share in a business to meet those claims.

Yes, there is a will – but what about insurance, pension, inheritance tax?

Many people think that by making a will and sorting out who gets what, they have removed all likelihood of problems after their death. More often than not and especially in the case of small businesses, they have not.

Insurance, pensions and inheritance tax can all threaten the immediate financial security of a business. These matters can change from year to year and you need to get professional advice from an accountant or financial adviser specialising in these fields to protect yourself against future eventualities. Don't delay – you need plenty of advice and planning to deal satisfactorily with these complex issues.

Health and safety

Every business has different needs in the field of health and safety, and different Acts of Parliament deal specifically with offices, shops, factories etc. The Health and Safety at Work Act 1974 deals with *all workplaces*, and general safety issues and obligations, whatever the type of work being undertaken. These include adequate toilets and washing facilities, machines that are electrically safe, protective clothing or equipment, precautions when using chemicals, and keeping your workforce clean and tidy.

The Health and Safety Executive (HSE), which is responsible for enforcing the law on health and safety at work, has plenty of leaflets listing questions for people running a small business. For example:

- Have you considered the risks to your employees?
- Do you know what to do if things go wrong – accident, fire or other dangerous occurrence?
- Are your arrangements for first aid satisfactory?
- Are you registered for health and safety purposes with the Health and Safety Executive or your local authority?

Even if you work on your own as a sole trader, or only employ one person, you should still think carefully about your workspace, and whether electrical switches and plugs are safe – are they too near piles of paper, for instance? Is your electrical equipment out of reach of your children?

The HSE has set up Health and Safety Small Firms Advisory Services – phone numbers vary around the country – so you can get advice. The HSE phone number and address are at the back of this book in Checklist 4.

Maternity pay

Maternity pay and maternity leave entitlements in Britain have been very complicated for many years, and were previously only available to women working for two years full-time or five years part-time, for the same employer. But all this changed in October 1994 when, in order to comply with the European Community Pregnancy Directive, any woman employee with more than 26 weeks' service by the due date of her baby's birth is entitled to a legal minimum of 18 weeks' paid maternity leave with 6 weeks at 90 per cent of her income and 12 weeks' Statutory Maternity Pay (SMP) at a rate based on sickness pay.

A woman is entitled to a total of 40 weeks' maternity leave altogether, but many women will only be paid for the 18 weeks' minimum. Some women are not entitled to SMP but to a lower payment called maternity allowance.

The law is still very complicated, and both benefits to employees and repayments by the government to employers can be lost if deadlines are not met or complied with.

Employers can claim 92 per cent of SMP from the government and small employers within the scope of Small Employers Relief for Statutory Sick Pay can claim 100 per cent of SMP.

It is best to get advice either as an employer, or an employee, from your local Citizens' Advice Bureau, Department of Social Security or the Maternity Alliance. Addresses and phone numbers are in Checklist 4 at the back of this book.

Equal pay

Since 1970, the Equal Pay Act has made it unlawful to pay different wages to men and women doing the same or broadly similar work. In addition, since 1984, anyone doing work of equal value to that of a colleague of a different sex, but paid less, or not getting the same terms of employment (for instance, the opportunity to work overtime or to claim sick-leave and paid holidays) can make a claim for equal pay.

A famous case involved a female cook working in a shipyard canteen who, in 1988, successfully proved that although she was paid less than skilled men working in the shipyard, her work was of equal value to theirs and should be paid equally. After taking her case right through to the House of Lords, she eventually received a pay rise of £24 a week and back pay, which together totalled £5340.

Although this law was brought in with the main intention of correcting inequalities in pay for women, it is not for women only. It gives the same right to a man to claim equal pay with a female colleague, if a man feels he is not being paid equally.

Sex discrimination

A person does need to be in employment to make a complaint under the Sex Discrimination Acts of 1975 and 1986. A complaint can be made whether someone is still working for an organisation or not. For instance, if a women is made redundant, and only women workers have been made redundant while male workers have been kept on, she may have a case for claiming unlawful sex discrimination.

Workers can also claim sex discrimination if made redundant because of pregnancy, or if they feel job interviews or recruitment procedures discriminate against them – for instance, someone who fails to get a job and believes that, because she was a woman, she was asked questions about their family life and childcare arrangements which were not asked of male applicants. Workers can also make claims about sexual harassment.

Racial discrimination

It is unlawful for employers to treat people differently because of their ethnic or racial origins, and this can apply to policies on recruitment, pay, staff benefits, training, promotion, working conditions and the awarding of contracts. The Commission for Racial Equality may provide legal and financial help in fighting cases.

There are three legal definitions of racial discrimination.

- *Direct discrimination,* for instance, refusing to recruit or promote people because of their colour, or ethnic or racial background.
- *Indirect discrimination,* for instance setting conditions of work which people from particular ethnic groups cannot fulfil or comply with for cultural or religious reasons. This could include the compulsory wearing of skirts as part of a uniform for women workers or compulsory wearing of hats for men who wear turbans.
- *Victimisation,* for instance, sacking or penalising someone because they have made or supported a complaint of racial discrimination against an employer.

Exceptions

Laws on race relations and discrimination do not apply to jobs undertaken wholly or mainly abroad, or to employment in private houses. In addition, selection on racial grounds is *not* unlawful if there is a genuine link between the job and a particular racial background, for instance recruitment of a waiter or waitress only of Chinese origin for a restaurant serving Chinese food, or selection of an actor or actress for a role requiring someone of a particular colour or racial origin.

For further information or advice contact the Commission for Racial Equality – address in Checklist 4 at the back of this book.

Further information and advice

Free information on the Equal Pay and Sex Discrimination Acts for both employers and employees is available from JobCentres and other offices of the Employment Service, and from the Equal Opportunities Commission – address in Checklist 4 at the back of this book.

Legal aid is not available for these cases because they are heard at industrial tribunals and not in courts. In theory, industrial tribunals are open to anyone to argue their own case without a lawyer.

It is worth noting that many successful cases under the equal pay, sex discrimination and racial equality laws are backed by trade unions, which often do not operate in small businesses. However, both the Equal Opportunities Commission and the Commission for Racial Equality back cases themselves where they feel the case is strong enough. In addition, law centres may take up cases free of charge to the claimant.

VAT

VAT is a tax levied by all the governments of the European Community on services. In the UK, it is payable to the government department called Customs and Excise and is currently at 17½ per cent. The tax is payable quarterly for small businesses and quarters are set individually for each business depending on the date of registration. Large businesses may pay VAT monthly.

VAT is an indirect tax, which means everyone who buys a VAT-rated service has to pay it on top of the bill. For instance, you have to pay VAT on telephone bills, whether you are VAT-registered or not. Once you are registered for VAT, you can offset this VAT against the VAT you receive.

You can register for VAT as an individual, a sole trader, a partnership, a company or a co-operative.

VAT – watch the VAT threshold

The VAT threshold is set by the government and VAT is administered by the Customs and Excise Department. When your turnover reaches around or above a set amount per quarter you are legally bound to charge VAT on your goods and services. You don't have to wait until your turnover is over the limit, you can register when you are approaching the limit and you can stay registered even if your turnover goes below the limit.

You can register as a freelance on your own using your own name or a business name, or as a partnership or company. Once you are registered you set up your accounts to suit your quarterly VAT returns, you can charge VAT on your services and claim it back on bills from other people who are charging you VAT. You'll have heard comments about VAT and some of the faintly ridiculous things on what is VATable and what isn't, but while it's true that VAT as a whole *is* a vastly complicated topic, *you* only have to know the general principles in your own field of business and most people can grasp that fairly quickly.

Your local Customs and Excise office, and your accountant or book-keeper can explain the details to you.

VAT came into effect on 1 April 1973 and the VAT threshold used to be relatively low so that a lot of freelances and self-employed people had to charge VAT on their goods and services either as soon as they started trading or very soon afterwards. However, in recent years the VAT threshold was raised by the government so that it did not affect as many small business enterprises.

The current threshold is now set at well over £40,000 per year, so you need a turnover of at least £10,000 a quarter before you have to start thinking about whether or not you need to register for VAT.

Currently, if you are a freelance working as a one-person business, you may never need to worry about whether to register for VAT or not. If you are a partnership, or a company with two or three people or more, you are more likely to need to find out if your turnover is approaching the limit and you may have to register for VAT.

The *advantage* of registering for VAT, and of staying registered even if your turnover drops, is that VAT registration implies a certain level of business and turnover, and you may wish to continue charging VAT as part of your image as a successful businessperson.

The *disadvantage* of VAT registration can be that if you are a one-person business competing against other one-person businesses who are not VAT registered, you may find they beat you on prices and you lose out by staying registered if you don't legally have to.

When you register, you receive a VAT registration number which should appear on all your own invoices to clients or customers on which you are charging VAT. This is because some of your clients or customers will themselves be registered to pay VAT and they will use your invoices in their own accounts.

VAT is levied by Customs and Excise and is completely separate from income tax, capital gains tax, inheritance tax, and corporation tax, all of which are levied by and payable to the government via the Inland Revenue.

If your turnover comes within a few thousand pounds of the VAT threshold, you are advised to register for VAT, because if you go over the VAT limit – either annually or in one trading quarter – you will have to pay up anyway. If your are not registered, you may not have kept all the relevant bills on which you have paid VAT, and which you could offset against the VAT paid to you.

If you do have a VAT accounting system in place, whereby you are balancing plus VAT against all your business expenses where VAT is charged to you, you will end up paying less to Customs and Excise. This is because what you have to do is add up the VAT you have received in one column, add up the VAT you have paid out on business expenses in another column and pay the difference to Customs and Excise.

General advice on VAT is available from your local VAT office which is listed as 'Customs and Excise' in the phone book. Your accountant or book-keeper can give you a system for keeping your accounts and basic information about how VAT works. In addition, Training and Enterprise Councils can offer free advice and, if you join them, you can get detailed advice from the Federation of Small Businesses, chambers of commerce, and professional and trade organisations covering your area of business.

Simple specimen VAT account for one quarter

Left hand page – general heading

Outputs – From *(date on VAT tax return)* **To** *(date on VAT tax return)*

(**Your business name** plus number of quarter)
For example 'Mega Cookie Company 1st Quarter, 1st Year'

Column headings

DATE	DETAILS	INV. NO. (short for Invoice Number]	TOTAL INC. VAT	NET OF VAT	VAT
1/01/95	Contract with American Cafe	1	£117.50	£100.00	£17.50
3/01/95	Cookies supplied to Catering Col. Ltd	2	£352.50	£300.00	£52.50
	TOTALS		£470.00	£400.00	£70.00

You should have a numbered invoice book with carbons to record your services on which you have charged VAT for your outputs, so you can easily separate the figures for each column. For inputs, however, you may have some receipts which only have the final total paid and don't have the VAT. In this case, the formula to find the current VAT rate of $17\frac{1}{2}$ per cent is to take the total and multiply by 7/47 i.e. multiply by 7 and divide by 47. You write your own invoice numbers on the input receipts as you enter them, clip them together and keep them in an envelope for each quarter.

Simple specimen VAT account for one quarter

Right hand page – general heading

Inputs – From *(same date)* **To** *(same date)*

Mega Cookie Company 1st Quarter, 1st Year

Column headings

DATE	DETAILS	INV. NO. (short for Invoice Number]	TOTAL INC. VAT	NET OF VAT	VAT
1/01/95	name of supplier 50 kg flour	1	£58.75	£50.00	£8.75
2/01/95	name of garage petrol	2	£20.00	£17.02	£2.98
	TOTALS		£78.75	£67.02	£11.73

To find out how much VAT you need to pay, you **subtract** the VAT on **inputs** from the VAT on **outputs**. In the simple example given here that means £70–£11.73 = £58.27. So you have to write a cheque for that amount payable to Customs and Excise, and send it off with the quarterly VAT return. If you are making a loss in a quarter and the VAT on inputs exceeds outputs, you can claim for a refund of VAT.

The heart of the VAT system are its twin pillars, inputs and outputs. VAT deals mainly with inputs and outputs, though there is another wrinkle called **zero-rating**. Also, if you do work for companies abroad and within the European Community, you need to account for these separately on your quarterly form.

VAT and the logic of cricket

There are many legendary tales of the idiosyncracies of the VAT system but the most obvious are the definitions of inputs and outputs. VAT suits product producers and retailers who buy in things – **inputs** – and sell them on as products or parts – called **outputs**.

For many service industries VAT means that what you receive in fees – what you you and I would class as **income** is known in VAT terminology as **outputs**. Meanwhile, conversely, what in a service industry are the business expenses and outgoings – such as rent, stationery, phone calls, petrol, vehicle expenses and business equipment – are classed as **inputs**.

So to sum up, for VAT purposes:

- what you **get in** are **outputs;**
- what you **spend out** are **inputs**.

The VAT system has its own impenetrable logic and terminology, and it's best to allow your accountant or book-keeper to exert their brain cells on its finer mysteries.

What you need to do is simply to accept your fate and draw up your VAT accounts – whether you write them out by hand, or type out your VAT account on a word processor or computer – with the correct labelling of outputs and inputs.

Remember, Customs and Excise have the legal powers to come and look at your VAT accounts at any time. VAT inspectors have absolute powers to enter your home or office whenever they feel something needs their expert attention.

Disadvantages of VAT

VAT is seen by some small businesses and self-employed people as a barrier to expansion and competitiveness, and some people deliberately keep their turnover and business small to avoid becoming liable and so having to charge customers extra. This is particularly relevant in service industries, where a number of small operators abound. For instance, plumbing, decorating, building work, car repairs and secretarial services are just a few examples.

The problem is that, for a small operator, the extra cost of VAT on each bill may be the difference between getting orders and not getting them. Competitors who don't charge VAT will be offering cheaper bills to the customer.

Advantages of VAT

On the other hand, some small businesses see VAT as an asset. They keep their VAT registration even though they could deregister when they're below the turnover limit, because they believe that staying registered makes them seem more prosperous. In other words, if they're still registered for VAT, it implies they have a turnover around or above the VAT limit.

It can also be useful to stay registered even if your turnover falls or you form another business and divert some of your previous turnover, because the discipline of the system makes you keep your accounts up to date – at the very least, you have to do your accounts every three months and if you're not naturally a financially well-organised person, even that reckoning, spaced out at the end of a quarter, provides a shape for your business and its accounts.

Others who are very much better organised and able to sort out their accounts week by week will manage perfectly well without needing the VAT discipline to keep them in line.

From an admin point of view VAT can be a nightmare, but from a cash flow point of view it can be an advantage, because it's money you can hold onto for about three months.

Colin Murphy, the Bookkeeping Bureau

Data Protection Registration

If you keep names and addresses of clients in a computer, you may have to register under the Data Protection Act. It sounds very broad but you may keep names and addresses in a computer – and who doesn't nowadays? – and still have no need to register.

The main aim of the Act is to prevent misuse of private

information and protect mailing lists in an age where computer technology makes swift information transfer and mailings to millions of people everyday occurrences. Small businesses used to have to fill in a vast form without much relevance to the day-to-day running of their business and its one or two computers.

However, there is now a pack specifically for small businesses, and if you think you might need to register you can send off for it and make your own assessment before paying to register. See Checklist 4 at the back of the book.

Split boards, and partnerships

Whether a split in a company board or partnership arises because of personal or professional differences, the effects can be devastating on a small business. Often it may be impossible to avoid some difficulties while a settlement is worked out and, at the worst, both partnerships and limited companies have ended up in court to try to settle their differences over who owns which part of the business. Legal advice may be necessary even if things do not get as far as court cases because legal rights are involved if assets and goodwill are to be split up.

Family businesses

Many businesses are family businesses, and they derive both strengths and weaknesses from their family base. The strengths come from people knowing and trusting each other, and working well together. The weaknesses come from people knowing each other too well, and allowing family values and attitudes to colour their business decisions.

For instance, the basic difference between employing someone you are related to and someone you are not related to is in what you expect from them. With a relative you are employing them because they are there, and then you build a job around them and their need for an income. With someone unrelated you want to train them to fit into your organisation and its needs. You can see that the standpoints and the positions you approach from are therefore completely different.

Sometimes you may make decisions based on business principles, sometimes based on family principles. You have contradictory influences right from the start. The personal has to be distinguished and separated from the professional, and this is especially true with husbands and wives.

The family business can have great potential for success, but it can also have built in problems which may not be apparent at the start but will come charging out of the forest just when a new deal is about to be signed – and always at moments when you least need them.

Expert advice on family business is available, and there is a newsletter run by accountants and business advisers, Stoy Hayward, who run the Stoy Centre for Family Business in London. See the Checklist 4 at the back of this book.

Financial safety checklist

1. Check your business insurance – is it up to date in value?
2. Do you need key worker insurance?
3. Check your pension – is it in trust?
4. Check your life insurance – is it in trust?
5. Check your home insurance – is it up to date in value?
6. Make sure you have a will – is it up to date?
7. Get advice on inheritance tax.
8. Make sure you have an agreed procedure for dealing with disputes with business partners or directors.
9. Think through any divorce implications if you have business partners or directors married to each other.

5

Getting Going – Where and How

—■—

The golden rule is that there are no golden rules.

George Bernard Shaw

LOCATING YOUR BUSINESS

THERE'S AN OLD SAYING among estate agents that there are three key factors which matter when selling a property. The first is location. The second is location. And the third is – yes – location.

For some businesses, location may be the key crucial factor which makes the big difference to the success or failure of the whole show. But this does not mean that all businesses have to be in prime expensive locations. You may be running your business from your home in the suburbs or in the country, yet you make all your deadlines and meet people when you need to without strain. Your location is not holding you back – in fact, it's giving you a competitive advantage because of low overheads.

But if you are running your business from home and you frequently get stuck in traffic rushing to the centre of your city, which often makes you late for appointments, the location of your office at home may be less than ideal. It may actually be costing you more in goodwill than you are saving in rent. On the other hand, if you are renting an office in the city centre which is so expensive you are barely making a living at all, that prime location may not really be paying its way. It might be better to look for a desk, or a couple of desks, in someone else's expensive office and ask them to licence it/them to you.

Licensing workspace

A licence is a way of obtaining workspace without the cumbersome agreements and long-term notice on either side that are needed if you take a lease. Most licences are on a month's notice on either side and give small business ventures the opportunity to get started without too much capital outlay but with the flexibility to move fast if necessary.

Buildings which are run as business centres for small businesses on licence usually offer some common services, such as the use of meeting rooms, photocopiers, receptionist to take messages etc. If you are offered a licence without any of these services, you may need to compare the office you are looking at with other licensed offices before committing yourself.

Licences – for and against

For:
- flexibility;
- fewer overheads;
- can move quickly if necessary.

Against:
- lack of privacy;
- lack of space;
- no long-term security.

CASE HISTORY:

A Licence to Make Money

Subject	Colin Murphy
Current role	Sole trader, The Bookkeeping Bureau Ltd (limited company) and Eurostudy (sole trader)
Nature of business	The Bookkeeping Bureau bridges the gap between routine book-keeping and full financial management. Eurostudy sells language courses abroad
Location	Chiswick, West London
Hours worked	At least 50 hours a week: 'I suppose on average I get in at 8 a.m. and work until 6 p.m. or 6.30 p.m.; occasionally I work at weekends. We have one client who requires us to be at a meeting at 6 o'clock in the morning every Tuesday'
Employees	2
Turnover	The Bookkeeping Bureau – £100,000; Eurostudy – £5000
Advertising/ marketing	Door drop brochure locally in Chiswick each year, plus word of mouth. Colin did use the local paper once to advertise but he says it did not produce much response

COLIN MURPHY, started his book-keeping business in August 1990 in a 'grotty little office' on Chiswick High Road, and moved into the barley Mow Centre in July 1992: 'I was paying £60 a week in the other place. I started with a licenced desk and now I have a licensed office.

'There are two types of office here – one where the partitions are shoulder high and there's not a lot of privacy, and self-contained offices. I started on my own with 50 ft² office space, then in January 1993 expanded when I took on an employee; with two of us working, a lot more work came in and we were holding a lot of private information. So in June of that year we moved into a private office with our own key. Now I have 150 ft² and I'm still a licensee.

'It's very sociable here at the Barley Mow, so things like getting up in the morning and going to work are easier. There are people to chat to, and more incentive as you get the advantage of working in an office atmosphere but without the office politics. It's much better than going to a grotty office on your own. Another advantage is that if half my client base were wiped out, or if I doubled it overnight, I could move within the building without having to change my address or phone number. I've already moved twice in effect, but stayed within this building.'

Colin worked in the accounts departments of three companies before being made redundant in 1986. He then had various temporary book-keeping jobs: 'And that's when I started to get the feeling that there are a lots of people who aren't getting the best value from a book-keeper. If the companies were run properly, they wouldn't need temps to come in and sort them out,' he says. 'In addition, if their financial information had been up to date, they would be able to make better decisions.'

Q. *What are the best and worst things about being self-employed?*
A. Because I work with two other people, if I started strolling in at 9.30, they would too. So you're under pressure to take the lead when it's your business. But I do enjoy that. The job itself is not that exciting, but if you get a new client and cash flow's improving, then work is quite exciting.

Q. *How do you see the future?*
A. Even larger businesses now need to think smaller and look more closely at the people they serve. Whatever you're selling, you need to be based near the people you're selling to, so you know what's going on. Small businesses are the way forward – but only if they manage their finances properly. In this country, people think too locally. They should be selling in Europe or worldwide.

Q. *What advice would you give to others?*
A. I would strongly recommend moving into a business centre

because of the social aspect of being with lots of other smaller businesses; you can learn from them and also get customers. And don't go out and buy state-of-the-art office furniture or powerful computers – it's a waste of money. Get something basic with the software you need and get going.

Working without an office

There are always some people with that extra bit of flair and nerve who manage to set their business up on nothing and, although it looks like they're going into the middle of nowhere, they still end up well off and prosperous.

'When I first started in the confectionery business,' says Jan Morgan, now an estate agent running her own company, Grosvenor International, 'I didn't know much about it, so I worked out that the best place to aim a new business is in the middle of the market. If you aim too high, the big boys know too much, and they soon suss you out and expose your ignorance. The little people ask millions of questions and take up lots of time, and they expose you too. But the men – and I mean the men – in the middle are too busy trying to climb higher, so they don't want to lose face and look stupid by asking you questions. You put on a front that implies you know what you're doing and they *never* ask questions. They play the game and sign the deals.

'And that's exactly what happened to me. I went to the World Sugar Fair with only my one *spiel* and my few bits of background knowledge, and the first man I talked to bought the deal I wanted. I'd asked someone who knew, "What's a middling amount of glucose to sell?" And he replied "100-ton lots". So, aiming at the middle of the market, that's what I arranged to import, and it worked. That first man to sign a contract with me never even asked what the price was; he just assumed it would be right because I was playing the game and talking his business language and being businesslike.'

Jan is famous among her friends for having started her confectionery business without any office at all. She is proof that if you calculate your market and your customers, and keep on the move, you can get away with – and accomplish – a lot.

'My customers were from abroad, so I could say to them, "My

office is in the suburbs, but I'll be in Central London on the day you want to meet so I could fit you in with my other appointments". I couldn't have got away with it with British people, who'd know that you just don't have offices in the suburbs! Of course, when I started I had no other appointments, but if you pick the right hotel (for example, the Coffee Shop at the Churchill – not too upmarket, not too downmarket, neutral not flashy decor) you can pitch the idea to them that you're very businesslike and busy, and they're very lucky to get some of your time.

'You have to get the right hotel, though – and it's not just the decor. It mustn't be too busy or the waiters might want to chuck you out – and the tables should be well spaced so you can have discreet business conversations. You can have an awful lot of free office space for the price of a few cups of coffee and some biscuits.'

Rent-free accommodation

If you are offered rent-free accommodation for your new business, it might sound like an offer you shouldn't refuse. 'Just give me the chance', you're saying as you read this; 'I should be so lucky.' But, just as there's no free lunch, there's also no totally free office.

There are always hidden disadvantages as well as the obvious advantages in this kind of deal. The first and most obvious question is: Why are they offering me this deal? Is it because they want to have a free receptionist by using my secretary to answer everyone else's calls when they're out? 'You won't mind us switching the calls through, will you? After all, you *are* here rent free.' Note that last phrase: another disadvantage of rent-free accommodation is that they never let you forget it. Even if they are discreet and it's never spoken out loud, it's there all the time: they think you're not as good as other tenants.

Are they giving you a rent-free deal because you're a threat to their business and they can nullify your competition by getting you in their building or their main office and tying you to using their facilities, not a rival's? If that's the deal, it may be rent free but it's costing you money – money you're paying to them.

Finally, the worst disadvantage of not having a proper rental agreement is that you have no security; you can be chucked out any time without notice – not a happy thought.

Rent free? There's always a reason, and advantage for the people making the offer. And it may not cost you rent but it may cost you sleepless nights. It may suit you to take up an offer of rent-free accommodation for a short time, but as soon as possible you should regularise your position as a tenant or move on.

Setting up a shop

High streets are not currently short of empty shops. A combination of a double whammy of recession and trade being sucked into out-of-town superstores has forced retailers, new and old, experienced and inexperienced, to close down all over the UK. But running a shop, like running a pub, is still a dream for thousands of people and many still plunge in without any retail experience at all.

One way to reduce your financial risks is by taking on a franchise with a ready-made, tried-and-tested business concept. You can buy an existing shop, provided you have worked out how you can turn it into a nice little earner. Or you can take the riskiest gamble of all – open your own shop with a new format and no past record to rely on.

Location is always a key factor in running a shop. Being in the right place for passing trade can be the difference between success and failure. Always research your preferred shop, whether it's empty or a going concern. Running a shop can be a big adventure whatever you're selling – but, as with other business ventures, it won't be any fun at all if you don't plan ahead.

Points to watch

- How good is the location in terms of adding to custom?
- How much passing trade is there?
- What is the competition?
- What are the opening hours and should you extend or reduce them?
- Whether you're buying a going concern or setting up from scratch, what services or products will you offer which are not being offered now?
- How many people will you need to employ?
- Does the shop need refitting?

- How much will it cost to refit the shop?
- Will you need a bank loan?
- Do you know the law? Contact your Local Trading Standards Office for information on the law and consumers' rights or subscribe to *Croner's Reference Book for the Self-employed and Smaller Business*. Contact the National Association of Shop-keepers – address at the back of this book in Checklist 4.

Workshops

You may be able to find subsidised workshops in areas where central government, local council or European Community funds have been used to build or renovate workspaces.

Contact your local Training and Enterprise Council to ask about this. Also the Scottish Office, the Welsh Office, LEDU in Northern Ireland or the ten urban regeneration offices in England – phone numbers can be found in Checklist 4.

Setting up a market stall

You wouldn't think it when you're watching *Eastenders*, where everyone always has time to chat and go off to the cafe, but running a market stall is very hard work. Apart from the fact that any successful selling involves a lot of preparation and effort, you don't have the luxury of a shop, so your stock has to move with you – and you have to move it. No wonder the beginners' advice from the National Federation of Market Traders stresses that a van – a reliable van – is vitally important.

But hard work and cold winds aside, there are many pluses to market stalls – in particular the fact that you don't have a shop, or expensive shelving or display units keeps your overheads down. You will have to start off in a market as a casual and may have to queue up to get a stall, but you can try out different markets and find out which ones work best for you in terms of volume of business and competition from other traders.

The early bird gets the turn on a stall and, if you stick at it, you can get one or more regular stalls or pitches – and, above all, you will be your own boss and able to make your own business decisions. If you want to be a market trader you will need a licence from your local council, which you should contact to find out which department deals with trading licences. It may be technical services in one council, planning or environment in another. For more information, contact the National Federation of Market Traders.

Trading licences

Many businesses need a licence to trade. Here is a list of some of them:

auctioneers	children's nurseries	fruit machines
betting shops	cinemas	hairdressers
bingo halls	theatres	(sometimes)
cafes and restaurants	employment agencies	ice-cream sellers
caravan sites	food manufacturers	market stallholders
mobile food shops	kennels	selling tobacco
nursing agencies	anyone selling petrol	scrap metal dealers
nursing homes	riding schools	snooker halls
pawnbrokers	selling fireworks	theatrical employers
pet shops	selling alcohol	

Working from home

Working from home used to be norm for the professional classes, and still is for some medical professionals like doctors, vets and dentists, many of whom use rooms in their own houses or flats as consulting rooms, and are paid as freelances or contract workers, not as salaried individuals.

The phrase 'living above the shop' is literally true for many thousands of small shopkeepers, who live in the flats above their businesses and it's become a general phrase for anyone with a workspace in the place where they live, even prime ministers living at 10 Downing Street.

In Charles Dickens's novel, *David Copperfield*, Betsey Trotwood takes her young nephew to meet her lawyer friend, Mr Wickfield, to talk about the boy's education.

'I have not come for any law,' she announces as soon as she arrives.

'Then it is the drawing room, not the office,' Mr Wickfield promptly replies, showing his distinction between personal and professional advice, and personal and professional spaces, and also illustrating that it was the norm for lawyers to have offices in their own homes in the eighteenth and nineteenth centuries.

Mr Wickfield's distinction is one everyone working from home should bear in mind, because you can only make such a distinction if you have your workspace properly and efficiently allocated.

Advantages of working from home

- No travelling time.
- No rent for office or workshop.
- Control over working hours.
- Access to work whenever you need it.

Disadvantages of working from home

- Possible professional isolation.
- Responsible for all bills.
- Responsible for all equipment maintenance.
- Responsible for organising your own time.
- Possible lack of exercise, leading to weight gain.

General guidelines for working at home

- Need for self-motivation.
- Need for self-discipline.
- Must like what you're doing most of the time.
- Must be able to sell yourself and your business.
- May still need paid childcare if you are working from home while your children are below school age.

How not to do it

You must have your own space, even if it's only one desk, table or workbench. All those stories of people working on the dining-room table and building up a multi-million-pound business may have a certain romantic appeal but it's an appeal that's strictly limited for most people when turned into everyday reality.

The truth is that if you have to keep moving your work around and even packing it away to make room for the rest of the family, you will find it hard to keep track of things. Just one desk, and a few drawers and files can be enough at the start, but it's a minimum you really need. It's better still if you can have your own room, even if it's the smallest spare bedroom. With a desk, chair, shelves and filing cabinet, you have the basics of office efficiency and the possibility of a phone extension or a phone line of your own for the business.

Home alone tips

Novelist and journalist Deanna Maclaren, the author of several romantic novels, says:

If you're working on your own, it's very important to dress properly – you shouldn't slop around in the dreaded jogging suit, looking like someone who's about to do the school run. You should present yourself properly at home because it's part of keeping up your self-confidence. If you pass a mirror and you look sloppy, this dents your confidence for making those key phone calls when you have to sound, and be, very professional. If you're a manager, you should look like a manager.

You spend a lot of your life on the phone, so the psychology of phone calls is very important. People often say you should try standing up to make important phone calls and that really does work. I know women who put on a hat to make important calls, because it makes them feel formal, or they apply lipstick and look in the mirror to make sure they're smart and ready for action.

A mirror is very important. You can look at yourself and see that you're smiling, and that means your shoulders are back and you're breathing correctly. Then you won't be timid and without confidence, but definite and decisive.

Never take important business calls in the bath or lounging on a bed – people always seem to be able to tell from the tone of your voice that you're not sitting properly at a desk. I got the news that my first novel had been accepted while I was cleaning my teeth and I was so excited I took the call immediately, and tried to sound very literary and composed with a mouthful of toothpaste. I'm older and wiser now, and have learnt more tricks of the trade – such as ringing people back!

Using your home as an office – the law and you

Planning permission

For many people working from home, this need not pose any problems at all. If all you are doing is using a phone/fax, a word processor or typewriter, and your work is mainly paperwork and phonework, without the need for a lot of clients to visit you, you should have no problems. However there is a wide variety of things you can do from home as a self-employed person and this is not a clear area for all types of business.

Andrew James and Sophie Chalmers, who together run *Home Run*, a newsletter for people working from home, sum up the position this way:

> *'The rule of thumb is that if people don't know you're working from home, and you never do anything to disturb your neighbours while working, you don't need to tell anyone. So the best advice is – don't give anyone cause for complaint and don't have a feud with your neighbours about anything so that they might want to cause you trouble. If your neighbours do complain about your business, then the local council has a duty to act and they are obliged to look at your business in terms of planning permission. Planning officers have great powers and the way they use them varies from council to council, depending on politics and planning policies within different areas. However, the main point is they can only respond to the public and, if they have no complaints, you can carry on your business not bothering anyone.*
>
> *'If you have to fight for planning permission, one useful*

technique is to have a visitors' book, and get every person who visits the house to sign it. If you have a family, you may get a lot of visitors anyway, and therefore you can show that in a typical month or couple of months, you had fewer business callers than domestic visitors.'

Planning problems

The main reasons why neighbours complain and you may need planning permission are as follows.

Parking   this is the number one complaint and reason for planning officers banning businesses from home – and you may have to make sure clients avoid parking too near your house by specifically asking them to park round the corner. This can pose very serious problems to your livelihood as a freelance worker from home.

Deliveries   if you set up a business requiring large lorries to make frequent deliveries and these are even more frequently collected by large numbers of small vans, you are not likely to be popular with your neighbours.

Noise   naturally people don't like noisy businesses, for instance metal beating, car engines or carpentry.

Smells   cooking for catering, hairdressing, repairing cars or motorbikes, making sauces or curries, curing leather etc. can all cause offensive smells and really get up your neighbours' noses. In addition all of these enterprises may come under Health and Safety Regulations or need licences to trade.

Business rates

This is also not a clear area for people working from home. If you use a separate room exclusively for business, technically you should pay business rates. However, if you can show that your computer is used by your children to play games, and/or if you have a spare bed or couch which turns into a bed in the room, then the room can be classed as a spare bedroom.

Garage or shed

Some famous authors, such as Daphne du Maurier and Roald Dahl, have worked in sheds in their gardens and have claimed they found inspiration in pulling on gloves and woolly hats, and switching on electric fires in the dead of winter. Not everyone takes this Spartan approach and you may wish to make your garage or shed into a 'proper' room with more home comforts than these two hardy novelists. There are some companies which now sell sheds specifically for use as home offices, and these are far less basic than the wooden hut which led to the creation of *Rebecca* and *Charlie and the Chocolate Factory*.

I know a violin teacher who has turned the garage of his Edwardian house into an office and music tuition room, and his local council had no objections provided the front of the house still looked as though the garage was still a garage. So, behind his non-opening garage doors, he has a room which, once you are inside the house, looks no different from any other room in terms of plaster, wallpaper, electric light and carpet. Because he has had to keep the garage doors on the outside, he has a window in the side of the 'garage' to let in more light.

The Royal Town Planning Institute sums up the position this way:

> *'If you live in a house and you use a garage or shed as an office, this is no different from using a bedroom or any other room as an office, and it's not going to interest the planners provided you don't interfere with other people. Of course, it's important to add that this does not apply if you live in a listed building conservation area, an Area of Outstanding Natural Beauty, or if you want to set up a factory or workshop employing people using machinery, and therefore the Health and Safety laws and other regulations are relevant.'*

If you want advice on planning, you can ring the Royal Town Planning Institute who can advise you how to find an independent planner in your area. The Institute's address and phone number are in the Useful Organisations list at the back of this book.

Do you need to check for parking standards?

If you are thinking of converting your garage and your property is a post-war property, you need to check with your council first to find out whether you are subject to planning conditions regarding parking standards. This means that your garage and/or drive are classified as parking units. The newer your house is the more likely it is to be subject to these regulations which are intended to maintain numbers of parking spaces and provide off-road parking. If this is a planning condition you need to apply for planning permission to change your garage.

Legal covenants – check your deeds

Some houses have covenants attached to the deeds which specify that certain activities are not allowed. For instance, some covenants forbid caravans and lorries from parking outside houses or flats. Removing these restrictive covenants where they exist is a legal matter between the property owner and the owner of the covenant. This will be defined in the deeds of the property. In practice many covenants are ignored, but if you find something vital to your work is restricted by covenant, can you rely on this? It's prudent to get legal advice from your solicitor if you are worried about covenants.

Home extensions

If you want to extend your home to create a workspace, you need to find out from your local council exactly how much you can extend without planning permission. Small home extensions are allowed without permission, but loft extensions and large additions to your home will require planning consent. If you can adjust your plans to come within the range of a small extension, then the same guidelines apply for extensions as for using existing rooms or garages. If you can't do this, you will have to allow extra time while your plans are scrutinised by the council planning officers.

If you live in a conservation area, an Area of Outstanding Natural Beauty or listed building, you will need planning permission for any home extension.

Useful tip – rent at least one BT phone

'It's important to rent at least one phone extension from BT,' says Sophie Chalmers of *Home Run*, because if you do, BT are responsible for all the phone wiring throughout your home as well as for replacing that phone if it goes wrong. In addition, for instance, if your office is upstairs, they are responsible for putting the wiring right through the house into the office, and also if there are any faults they come and repair them. If you don't hire anything from them, they simply bring the line to the front door and the rest is up to you.

'It's also worth bearing in mind that business lines are repaired quicker than domestic ones, so if something does go wrong with your phone line, you will be without it for much less time.'

CASE HISTORY:

The Listening Business

Subject	Celia Kemsley
Current role	Market Openings and Peak Performance
Nature of business	Market Openings is a management consultancy specialising in marketing strategy for service businesses, and has clients in both the UK and Europe. Peak Performance is a one-to-one counselling service for business people to discuss any issues affecting their efficiency at work
Location	Goodge Street, Central London
Hours worked	'I haven't a clue – I adapt my working hours to suit the circumstances'
Employees	Just Celia
Turnover	Not disclosed
Advertising/ marketing	Word of mouth and personal recommendations only

CELIA KEMSLEY is one of those open, friendly people who appears to
give a lot away; in fact, what she does is make other people open up
in response, so you soon find that *you're* the one giving away a lot.
It's a technique I recognise because journalists tend to use it – but,
unlike a journalist, Celia soaks up a lot of information and analyses it
without making it public. Discretion is her livelihood and confidential
reports are her bread and butter.

Working from her office in her flat in Central London, close to
Goodge Street Tube station, she has built a solid career over the past
ten years as management consultant, working on her own and without
a lot of formal training.

'I've had three different careers and I've started each one from the
bottom,' she says. 'I started as a secretary to a marketing manager,
then became a marketing manager in a textile agency, selling cloth in
bulk to people who make garments. Then I hovered on the brink of
freelancing for four whole years – I'd decided I wanted greater freedom
but I wouldn't take the plunge. Finally, things just developed, but in
completely different ways to those I had originally planned.

'I had thought I would do something like being a consultant on
new product development or putting energy into existing products,
but although I did get some work like that, I also got projects relating
to internal motivation within a company. This developed into what I
do now, which is about congruency within an organisation – making
what happens on the inside and outside go together.'

Celia's main business is her management consultancy, Market
Openings, but Peak Performance, her one-to-one counselling service
for business people, has grown out of it in recent years and she now
runs the two businesses separately.

'Peak Performance started when my existing clients asked me to
listen to them talking about their business problems,' she says. 'But
now I'm also getting clients who are completely new to me, because
word has spread about the usefulness of paying someone like myself who
can be an informed listener, and help to clarify and sort out problems.'

Celia has moved her own career sideways and upwards three times,
and her great strengths seem to be her openness to change and her
flexibility – qualities she believes everyone working on their own
should have and act upon: 'It's all very well going on courses to learn
how to put together a business plan or to keep useful records, but
you actually need to be *ready* to be a success at whatever you do. Be
clear about what success means to you. It may not be financial; you
may have other priorities. Luck is recognising an opportunity when it
presents itself, and acting on it. Learn to recognise the opportunities
that are going to mean *success for you*.'

Q. *What mistakes did you make at the start?*

A. I tried to be the way I thought a 'proper' management consultant should be and not simply be myself. I would deliver reports – weighty tomes that no one read – and then suffer because my clients didn't seem to take up my recommendations. I soon developed a style which is wholly congruent with who I am, and since then client relationships have been smooth running and mutually satisfying.

Q. *What are the best and the worst things about being self-employed?*

A. The best is freedom and there are two types. The first is the freedom to develop my work in whatever way gives me the most satisfaction. I sell ideas and new ways of looking at things, and I need the freedom to be self-employed to follow through on anything that seems important to me at any particular time. The other freedom is to be able to do things outside the work area. One year I went sailing for two months. I also belong to a choir which does several tours a year. In 1993, for instance, I went to Barcelona, Lille and Istanbul.

Because I work and live on my own, the isolation is the worst thing about being self-employed. I can get bogged down on my own and I need someone or something else to pull me out of the bog. So, if I have a day where I'm not meeting anyone, I make a point of talking to a friend, so I can keep a proper perspective on life, the universe and everything.

Q. *How do you see the future?*

A. I certainly have no intention of going back to working full-time for someone else. But I don't think everyone will be freelance – some people are completely suited to this way of life but others really cannot adapt to it. I think that once this period of economic turbulence has settled organisations will be more open to using freelance services than before the recession, but they will achieve their own maximum potential by developing a core group of people who share a common ethos and vision, and will insist on working with freelance people who carry an outlook in harmony with their own, and can bring in new skills and experience where required.

Q. *What advice would you give to others?*

A. My own best decision was to buy a personal computer when personal computers were not as familiar as they are now (even before IBM brought out their first model). Even though it was quite a struggle to familiarise myself with it, just owning a computer enabled me to take on projects which I would otherwise have found great difficulty in accomplishing.

Also, it's a great idea to join groups where you can meet people who may either be useful contacts or who will simply keep you sane at times of high stress and isolation. I joined both Women in Management and Network, a group for senior professional women, ten years ago, and belong to three other professional groups.

BUSINESS EQUIPMENT

'The best thing is to start small and *not* lash out loads of money on expensive equipment which you may not need,' says Barbara Kidd, managing director of Herforder UK, sole UK agent for a German carpet and flooring company. 'You don't know what you really need until you get started and then everything becomes a lot clearer and you can buy things as you go along.

'If you're working from home, it's a very economical way to operate because you don't have travel costs, rent and other bills, so it's stupid to waste money on stuff you won't be using. Whether you're working at home, or in a space you're paying for, you need to grow organically, not artificially.'

Basic business essentials

It helps if you have a hole puncher and a lever arch file for your accounts, so it's easy for you to write things down every day, and file invoices and receipts as they occur. Files, notebooks and diaries are also very handy for listing your answerphone messages, mail received and work ordered.

There are no rigid rules about how you sort these out, but you do need to sort out a system for your paperwork and use routines to keep track of your work, your expenses, your income, and written and verbal messages and information received.

Daybook

The first and most important piece of stationery to buy yourself is a daybook. This can be bound or spiral bound, but most people find a bound notebook up to A5 size is the most useful. The purpose of this vital book is to write down what you need to do each day. But also, and more importantly, for you to write down all your messages, who rang you, what they said and their phone number, and your notes of business meetings and agreement of terms for work, and so on and so on . . .

I've written this in a long, breathless sentence because when you start up you often find that things move fast and small scraps of paper with important phone numbers get lost very fast. If you have everything written in a daybook, you can keep track of things and, most importantly you can find exactly what was discussed about payments and work required, and so avoiding some sticky problems with awkward customers. Once you've finished one day book you label and date it, keep it in a drawer so you can refer to it if necessary and start another one.

Stationery

- Large desk diary with one page a day.
- Notebook for mail, answerphone and phone messages.
- Cashbook.
- Sales daybook.
- Purchase daybook.
- Stapler, pens, paperclips.
- Six box files.
- Packs of plain paper for typing or printing from word processor.
- Small and large envelopes for letters.
- Headed paper, compliment slips and business cards.

Furniture

- Desk or table.
- Comfortable office chair.
- Filing cabinet.

■ Cupboards.
■ Shelves.

Basic technology

■ Phone.
■ Answerphone.
■ Fax with photocopying facility. (Phone, answerphone and fax can be combined in one machine which also has a photocopying function that's useful for a small amount of photocopying.)
■ Electronic typewriter with word processing.
■ Calculator.

More technology (optional for some; necessity for others)

■ Two or more phone lines.
■ Computer and printer.
■ Modem.
■ Mobile phone.
■ Photocopier.

Modern technology is on your side

The key to success for many freelances running small businesses nowadays is the technology now available to provide you with extra resources to take and receive recorded and written messages, and vital business information.

If you've never had to think about the installation and running costs of phone lines, answerphones, fax machines, mobile phones, computers, modems, printers, personal electronic organisers and photocopiers, you need to know.

Phone lines

Every business needs its own phone line. Call 152 to organise a new business line or 150 for a new residential line.

You might decide to keep your existing home line as your business line because so many useful people already have your number when you start trading. You might decide you need a new business line with a new number when you start working for yourself. Whatever you decide to do, it doesn't cost as much as you think.

If you're really strapped for cash or you don't share your home with other people, especially children, you can manage to run a small business with one phone line and you may decide not to invest in another phone line. But you should consider investing in an answerphone and possibly also a phone/fax machine, both of which can receive messages while you are out.

There are also many services now available from BT and Mercury which offer help to small businesses. You should look at phone services like call waiting, detailed billing and differing charge structures, and work out which ones can help you. Do you need a mobile phone? For some businesses this will be an expensive luxury, while for others, particularly those who travel during their work, it will be a necessity.

Telephone tips

When I first started operating from home, more than 12 years ago, using a desk, an office chair and shelves along one wall of my bedroom, things were much more strict and straitlaced than nowadays. By that, I mean that people working within organisations were much less open to freelances than they are now. They couldn't grasp that people could work professionally from home and they were less open to enquiries unless you gave the name of the organisation you were working for.

For instance, if I was writing a feature for a newspaper, I would ring and say I was Roz Morris from that paper – implying I was on the staff. I would never say I was a freelance representing that organisation on that one occasion.

People used to be much more suspicious of freelances – not within journalism itself, where the concept of freelancing has been around for a long time, but outside that profession, when they were approached for information. I used to dread having to give my phone number to get people to call back, and hearing the change in their tone of voice as they took it down and realised I wasn't at the main office – where 'real' workers were based. 'I'm working from home today,' I used to state bravely, implying that I wasn't usually so humble and insignificant, and I really had a base within a big organisation.

Nowadays, it's perfectly satisfactory in professional terms for people to find out that you work from home, whatever kind of service you're providing. 'I'm in my office at my home' is not the kiss of death – but this must be said with a professional tone, never apologetically. Working from home is not second best, and you will find it harder to get business if you present yourself apologetically and with that underlying assumption. However, this greater acceptance doesn't mean you can allow other unprofessional, homebody or folksy practices to creep in and ruin your professional image.

Just because you work at home, it doesn't mean other people need to know your personal habits or routines. Ask yourself, would you think it professional if someone you were talking to on the phone started to talk about their childcare or the person who answered the phone told you to 'hold on, she's in the loo/coming out of the shower/putting the baby down now'?

Would you really care about these details? Would you be irritated at being expected to be involved in someone's personal problems? Would you feel this was professional behaviour? Would you feel either envious that they were able to be at home in daylight hours or contemptuous of someone not working in a 'proper' work setting? Whatever the reaction, would you feel your regard for this person's professionalism was increased?

All these things stop the professional flow, the atmosphere of work-focused efficiency you should be working hard to create. In a business meeting you don't want to know personal details about people you've only just met.

A telephone call is just another type of business encounter and personal details – while they may loom larger when working at home – are not going to increase your professional standing. Quite the reverse in fact, because they will give the impression to others, still in the straitjacket of professional business outside the home, that you are not speaking the same language, are not like them and are more interested in your home than your work.

Never allow:

- a baby – yours or someone else's – to be heard, even in the background
- a baby – yours or someone else's – to be heard in the foreground
- a dog/parrot/etc. – yours or someone else's – to be heard at all
- loud pop music to be heard in the background
- children arguing – yours or someone else's – in the background
- a child to answer your business line
- a child to be heard in the background
- children to interrupt you on a business call.

Never say:

- I don't know – my husband/wife/partner deals with that
- I don't know – I haven't a clue about finances
- I have to ring off now because I've got to feed the baby
- I have to ring off now because I've got to fetch the children from school
- I have to ring off now because the children have come home from school
- I have to ring off now because I've got to pay the milkman
- I have to ring off now because I've got to go to the loo/turn off the bath/shower/cooker
- I have to ring off now because I've got to cook the supper
- I have to ring off now because I have to go to the bank
- I can't talk now because . . . *add any of the above.*

If you are asked a question you can't answer, **don't panic – buy time**. Never say 'I don't know' – try saying:

- let me get the details on that and I will get back to you in five minutes (then ring someone else who does know the answer);
- that's very interesting – can you quickly fax me all the details of what you want?
- I'll get my colleague to get back to you straight away on that (then get someone else to ring who *does* know the answer).

Others should say:

- she/he's in a meeting
- she/he's just gone to a meeting
- she/he's with a client
- she/he's away from her/his desk at the moment
- she/he's out of the office all day
- she/he's out at the moment but back very soon.

Add to all of the above: Can I take a message?

To end a call, you should say:

- I have to ring off now because one of my clients is due
- I have to ring off now because I have to go to a meeting
- I have to ring off now because I've got a lot of work to get through before the end of the day
- I have to ring off now because there's a call waiting.

Telephone train that teenager

Yes, it is possible to have a teenager answer the phone in a professional manner and take a message accurately, with a telephone number for you to call back. Training is easier if the income generator using the home phone line is the household's first income – obviously everyone then needs to pull their weight or even eating will be at risk.

However, although a second income may not seem so obviously important, it may be the vital extra boodle that provides the difference between running a car or having a family holiday, or paying for ballet, riding, any extra leisure lessons, going to the cinema or not. And it is possible to get this over even to teenagers with their own self-centred perspective on life.

Your perspective here could include money for clothes, shoes, pocket money, teenage telephone bills, televisions in bedrooms, personal computer games, driving lessons and all those other terribly cheap expenses that teenagers like to regard as part of a normal lifestyle.

You will be taking on a lot, though, if you try to fight it out for the phone line with a teenager – or, worse still, more than one teenager, every day after school, and all day throughout the school holidays. You will never win, except at great personal cost. Much better to install your own business telephone line, right from the start.

Answerphones

Every self-employed or freelance person needs an answerphone. Even if you are office based, there will be times when you have to leave the office and that's always going to be the time when someone will call you, even if you've had no other calls all day. Answerphones are also acceptable professionally.

Answerphones help to maintain the professional flow, part of the aura of efficiency you need to build up to maintain your clients and your cash flow.

If you get an answerphone with a remote access device, you can ring your own phone, hear your own message and then use the device to bleep instructions to the answerphone. It will then play the messages received while you've been out and you can keep ahead of the game by ringing back today instead of tomorrow.

Your answerphone message

Beatle John Lennon was famous in his heyday not only for having an answerphone long before all the rest of us, but also for having the clear and unhelpful message: 'Hello, this is an answering machine which will not record your message. Click'. The phone then cut off.

How would your own message be marked out of ten? Sound quality? Background noise? Tone of voice? Paper rustling? Content? Tape quality? In short, this is one of your business lifelines. Does it sound old and frayed, and a load of old rope. Or is it clear, efficient and appropriate for the job?

Celebrities seem keen on using music before their voice is heard, perhaps not surprisingly if they are disc jockeys or childen's television presenters. But, unless you are in showbusiness in some way, music will not necessarily impress your clients, who may feel you are wasting their precious time with trivia while they wait to record their vital message.

Answerphone message do's

- Record your message with no background noise. Create an air of professional calm.
- For a recorded message on a business line, it is essential to state the business name first or your name if you are the business name. Most answerphone manufacturers supply an idiot's guide

to the kind of thing you can say in a recorded message and you can adapt it for your own needs.

A specimen message could be: 'Hello, this is Jane Smith (or Jane Smith Limited). No one can take your call at present, so please leave a message after the tone, giving the time of your message and a contact number, and we'll get back to you as soon as we can. Thank you for calling.'

Answerphone message don'ts

- For a recorded message on a phone line at your home, it is advisable not to give both your name and your number, just in case your caller is an unstable personality dialling calls at random from the phone book and likely to visit or burgle you later. Some people give the number but no name; others the name but no number.
- Don't leave a long gap before you speak on the recording. Callers may think they've been cut off and then put the phone down without leaving a message.
- Avoid machines with a dozen beeps before people can record their message. These can be irritating to callers – and waiting so long to speak results in them going into a kind of light coma and not waking up in time to record their message in the time available.
- Don't leave your machine on a long set of rings before the answering machine comes into action. Callers may give up and ring off. Not only will they not give any message, they will also be thinking you are so inefficient, tacky and small scale that you don't even have an answerphone. Two rings is enough for anyone and saves time for all your callers.

Some people are still irritated by any answering machine, but even they'll be less irritated by a quick, recorded response than a long set of rings which will get their hopes up of speaking to a real person.

Answerphone management

It is possible to handicap yourself even with all the advantages of an answerphone. Embarrassment and no increase in your professional standing follow if you ring someone whose voice is on your message tape, only to discover that they rang a week ago and 'One of your colleages has already rung me' or, worse still, 'You rang me last week about this – is the message *still* on your machine? *My* machine wipes messages automatically', etc.

Ways of avoiding this sort of drop in your business credibility include making sure you write down all messages and tick them when dealt with, erasing all messages, and generally taking the answer-phone seriously and giving it a place in your daily business routine.

Personal pagers

Basically pagers provide a one-way communication with a person while they are out of the office. If you want to contact someone who has a pager, you ring a number they have previously given you and then ask to give a message to a pager with a particular code number. Pagers can display messages of several words or they can simply bleep to tell someone to ring their base because there are messages. They then have to find a phone to ring from. Pagers are cheaper than mobile phones but may be less convenient for some businesses. The main pager operators are BT Paging, Mercury Paging and Vodapage.

Mobile phones

The market for mobile phones has grown very rapidly since the beginning of the 1990s as more and more people – particularly small business people working as plumbers, builders, and people who rely on travelling about to provide services or make sales – have realised their great advantages for acting fast in business. The phones have got smaller and so have the prices of the phones themselves, but the running costs are still currently much more expensive than a fixed phone line. So you need to know whether you can justify the expense and the monthly rental through generating extra business before you decide whether or not to sign up for one. There are also a number of competing services and it's worth finding one to suit your business. For instance, do you need a mobile to cover the whole country or would your business benefit from a cheaper service covering only a local area? Do you need a service which can give you calls abroad? Or would you just put a block on all foreign calls and so therefore you don't need this facility? Do you want an answerphone service? All the variations of service have different prices, so it's worth researching what's available and deciding exactly what ingredients you need before you commit yourself. Don't be put off by snide remarks from people without mobiles who almost certainly have no idea of the possible business benefits.

Answering services

You don't have to be a doctor on call or an actor waiting for work to find an answering service useful. If you're providing a service of any kind, you might want to consider the pluses of answering services.

The advantages are that clients know they can always leave a message for you day or night and that it will always be reliably reported to you – very valuable for business, especially business deals, in general, and particularly practical if you are working for or with people based abroad and with different time zones. Costs can be more reasonable than most people expect, especially when considering the potential costs of lost business. Answering services are usually listed in *Yellow Pages* with business names starting with Answer ..., and you should compare prices for services and find out if you know any of their customers or if they can give you the names of clients you can consult before making a decision.

Fax machine

The fax machine is one of the most important inventions in the past 20 years for all businesses, but particularly for small businesses. It enables information on paper to be sent around the world via phone lines. With it you can both send and receive information on a scale never previously thought of for small businesses. Without a fax you won't be really competing in a serious way for any kind of business.

You can fax business information to get sales, as part of your marketing and as part of your debt collection policy. If someone says they've lost an invoice, you can fax them another one – you don't have to accept those lame old excuses about things being 'lost in the post' or mislaid in the accounts department.

Photocopiers

Most fax machines have a photocopying facility, but this is very basic and you may need a photocopier as well. If so, buying or leasing secondhand may be the cheapest way of getting a good one. But make sure you don't sign a leasing agreement without reading it first and also getting your solicitor to read it. There have been problems with people signing agreements which bind them for lengthy periods into high payments. Many people find that their local print shop or post office supply cheap do-it-yourself copies. This may prove more economical if your usage is only occasional.

Personal computer

'In the 1960s I was working for a company where we bought the latest state-of-the-art computer and it needed a large room all to itself,' says Kenneth Lucas, now working as a freelance senior executive, known as an 'interim manager'. 'The computer itself cost £60,000, and the room to put it in had to be specially adapted and that cost another £60,000. This machine had 8 K of memory. I've got a calculator in my hand now that has 64 K. That's the scale of the changes we're talking about.'

Modern technology means small businesses can do the kind of work that medium-sized businesses used to do and medium-sized businesses can do the work of large ones. What does all this change mean to you? Are you using it in your administration and in your plans to tackle your potential market?

General equipment management

A very useful rule is to keep all the bumpf and file it somewhere you can find it easily. All the instruction manuals and guarantees, photocopies of receipts (originals go into your business accounts), maintenance and insurance details, and phone numbers of maintenance engineers and manufacturers, should be in a separate box file or drawer in your office. This should be clearly labelled and not used for anything else; there is nothing more frustrating than not being able to find vital details of equipment when it goes wrong and here I speak from experience. Not every crisis is a major one, and if you can find the instruction book you may work out what's wrong with your machine and put it right yourself.

Even if your machine has completely packed up, if it's still under the manufacturers' guarantee it won't cost you anything except your time. But to get repairs done under guarantee you need the receipt and the name of the shop where you bought it – details which can escape you and your filing system fairly fast while you're happily basking in the sunny security of machines that work perfectly.

Losing time is bad for the small business person because the phrase 'time is money' is never more true than when you're working for yourself and losing your time is losing your own money.

READY, STEADY GO

You've read this book so far, you've made plans, you've talked about them to people you trust. Here's a quick reminder of the steps you need to take to get started.

Step 1 Income tax

Inform the Inspector of Taxes for your district that you are now self-employed and wish to be on Schedule D or register your limited company at Companies House and inform the Inland Revenue that you will be paying yourself a salary. Get the relevant information from your local tax office.

Step 2 National Insurance

Inform your local Social Security office that you will be paying some or all of your National Insurance payments as a self-employed person or, if you're setting up a company, get the relevant information on deducting National Insurance from staff pay.

Step 3 VAT

Do you expect your turnover to be at or near the VAT trading threshold? Will you be purchasing a lot of supplies which are subject to VAT? You are allowed to register for VAT even when you are not close to the legal trading limit. Get the relevant information and leaflets from your local VAT office. Inform your local Customs and Excise (VAT office) if you are likely to need to register for VAT.

Trading tip

You can write instructing your accountant to do all this, if you think it easier and cheaper (in terms of your time) for him or her to do so.

Some people always throw up their hands and protest that it costs too much to get other people to do administrative work for you. But if you work out how long it will take you – starting from not even having the basic phone numbers and addresses – to find out the relevant correct information, type the letters, post them and then send copies to your accountant, you might decide it's more cost-effective to use your time on something where you're making money and use someone who has all this information at their fingertips to polish off all this admin in an hour.

If your accountant *can't* do this, is he or she the right accountant for you?

KEEPING UP WITH CHANGES

THERE ARE ALWAYS CHANGES to laws, rules and regulations, so how can you keep up? There are a number of things you can do, and they are all part of what you should be doing anyway to keep in touch with trends generally and in your own particular areas of expertise.

Read newspapers, trade newspapers and magazines, listen to the radio, watch television news and business programmes. Join organisations, like the Federation of Small Businesses, or your local chamber of commerce or trade or professional organisation. Get on free mailing lists for useful information from organisations, government departments or the European Commission. See the Checklist 4 at the back of this book.

Try to cast a rapid eye over all that bumf that comes regularly and relentlessly from the VAT people giving you details of VAT as applied to products and services you never knew existed. Before you file this in the waste bin, give it a quick look to see if there's anything relevant to you.

Above all, talk to other people running small businesses in your own field, and in others, about changes of all kinds, and learn from other people's experience. Getting a feel for trends is a valuable skill that can help you grow your business – and in some instances can help you preserve it – because you can spot what others miss or dismiss as irrelevant.

Businesses don't always evolve in a straight line, but often they move sideways into areas which start off as a small part of the whole business, and then grow and grow. Or they can suddenly leap into entirely new fields. But your business won't be able to leap if you don't keep on your toes.

At the start of this book I posed the question: 'When opportunity knocks – can your hear it?' This is not just a good question when you're starting up. It's a question that never goes away. Opportunities go on knocking – can you still hear them? And will you open the door and let them in?

6

Keeping Going

—■—

The Inner Game of Business ... is understanding the Business Paradox: the better you think you are doing, the greater should be your cause for concern; the more self-satisfied you are with your accomplishments, your past achievements, your 'right moves', the less you should be.

Mark McCormack, sport and show business agent, and head of International Management Group, in his book *What They Don't Teach You at Harvard Business School*

GETTING PAID

'A VERBAL CONTRACT ain't worth the paper it's written on.' These words are usually attributed to the legendary film producer Samuel Goldwyn of MGM (Metro Goldwyn Mayer), who was also credited with the line, 'I'll give you a definite maybe'.

Unfortunately, sharp practice is nothing new in Hollywood and it's nothing new in the rest of the business world either. So you need to have procedures not only to avoid relying on verbal agreements only but also to keep track of all payments and to try to track late payments down once you have identified them. This is not an area for drift and muddling through – this is where you need to keep your eye on the ball and not be deflected by elaborate excuses designed to slip things past you, and prevent you getting hold of your hard-earned money.

You need to be aware that there will always be some people who are determined not to pay promptly, and some who want to cheat you and deliberately behave dishonestly to avoid paying at all.

Here is the dirty dozen of common excuses.

1. 'The cheque's in the post.'
2. 'I can't authorise a cheque and the person who can is on holiday.'
3. 'Isn't that the deal where you gave us a credit note?'
4. 'We haven't paid that bill because we thought we had a discount.'
5. 'Our computer's down in the accounts department.'
6. 'Everyone in the accounts department has got flu.'
7. 'Everyone in the accounts department is on holiday.'
8. 'We've just changed our payments system, can you send another invoice?'
9. 'Your invoice wasn't correct.'
10. 'We're waiting for another invoice from you.'
11. 'We've just got a new computer in accounts and there's trouble with it.'
12. 'No, you'll have to send it again by post. We don't take faxed invoices.'

One of the oldest tricks is to send a cheque without a signature, a mistake which may not be noticed until the cheque reaches your bank, and is then returned and you still don't have any payment. If this happens, you might be well advised not to deal with a particular client or customer again, at least not without extracting payment in advance from them.

Some people will always be trouble and you will have to weigh up whether they are worth the bother they cause you, even if they do pay up in the end.

References

It is often the case that small businesses are so eager to get work that they forget about the simple business technique of asking for references before accepting contracts. This is a well-recognised business practice, and the usual procedure is to send a letter to a prospective customer asking them to give the details of their bank branch and account number, plus the names of two referees who have already done business with them.

Once you receive the names of referees, you must send them a letter detailing what you want to know – for instance, how long have they done business with the company, have they always paid their debts promptly, how much credit would you give them and would you recommend them as customers? You can also ask your bank to provide a status report on the financial viability of the company concerned.

If there are any problems, you may find a follow-up phone call will help. Understandably, people often don't want to put problems down on paper for fear of libel or other legal action against them.

If you have any doubts about a potential customer and you don't have time to take up references, you may be able to find out what you need to know by ringing friends or business acquaintances who have themselves dealt with the company or organisation concerned.

Precautions like these can prevent a lot of bother and loss of revenue in the future, especially where a large sum with an ongoing commitment and investment on your part is essential.

Money up-front

You can insist on money up-front if you are suspicious of a new client or an old one who has let you down before. You can make it your normal terms of business to get money up-front, so everyone knows where they stand.

Discounts for prompt payment

Offering discounts – small discounts of 5 or 10 per cent – for prompt payment may appear to cost you money, but if it brings in the cash quicker, it may be useful to you. However, you need to have a system you can keep track of so you know when people are no longer entitled to the discount. Some people find this too complicated to undertake when they start up; others run a tight ship with every invoice organised and dates for the end of discounts built in to the system from Day 1.

Debt collection

Most people who have ever had to chase other people for money develop routines to follow, so they can keep on top of these sort of problems. The first step in the routine is to have an efficient invoicing system, so you never end up wasting time contacting people to complain about non-payment, only to have them claim (truthfully) that they've already paid, (truthfully) that they've never received your invoice, (untruthfully) that they've never seen it or they've lost it. If you know your own system is efficient, you won't have to waste your phone bill ringing them a second time just to confirm that, yes, they have been sent the invoice.

You should make just one call – and have the relevant paperwork in front of you – and be prepared to send the invoice again immediately, by fax if possible.

Small businesses of all kinds usually end up with half a dozen late payments every year and many do manage to get all the money in the end. But there are no rules or predictable outcomes about this area of business and you may find that some payments are never made, either because the client has gone bust or moved away or because they query a bill and refuse to pay, and it simply isn't large enough to warrant your time in making the effort to get the money off them.

It is time that is the great enemy of debt collection where small debts are concerned. You may settle down to a whole morning or afternoon spent chasing people who owe you money, when, obviously, you may well think your time would be much better spent finding some new customers instead of chasing old ones who won't pay up.

You have to make the decision about when it's worth allocating time on phone calls, letters or faxes to remind organisations that they owe you money. All debts represent your work and your time which you've already sold, so taking time to chase debts is using time again – only this time it's unpaid.

For a large debt, some of your time is clearly needed to chase it up, but it should not be necessary to spend a lot longer on chasing a big debt than a little one. Have an efficient system and stick to it.

Debt checklist

1. Check your invoice – find the paperwork.
2. Always be ready to send the invoice again.

3. Always have a copy.
4. Always have a clean, legible photocopyable copy.
5. Fax a copy of the copy to the client.
6. Phone again to ensure the client has received the fax.

Is it your own mistake?

Sometimes it's your own fault that you haven't been paid. Have you forgotten to send the invoice? Have you sent the invoice but to the wrong department, perhaps in the wrong part of the country? Has this particular organisation got its own peculiar system for invoicing, so you have to fill in their form which they send to you and you've forgotten to send it back?

Dealing with late payments

Anything outstanding after 30 days is a late payment, but you must tailor your responses to your customers or clients. If you have a client who always pays up after about 40 days or even 60 days, and you can rely on that, there is obviously no point in wasting your resources on chasing these payments.

Tailoring your response can be far more effective than a blanket response which may be offensive to good customers who are regular payers. In some cases, an officious letter to the wrong customer or client may actually lose you some business.

What is the law on late payment?

Unfortunately, there are no laws in Britain setting time limits on business debts, although there are in other countries and the subject is being raised more and more frequently in political debate in Britain. Many business books assume that businesses are on a 30-day cycle for money flowing in and out of the business. In an ideal world, this would really be very nice and the pigs would be flying really well too.

Unfortunately, business surveys show that on average in Britain, payments are made 70 to 80 days after invoices are received. Any debt that reaches 90 days or more should be treated seriously, but it's better to allocate more time to chasing larger debts than smaller ones.

Unfortunately, small businesses are the most vulnerable in any situation where money is a long time coming. If you're a freelance you may be at the end of a long line of contractors and subcontractors, all of whom are waiting for the money to trickle down to them before passing it on. It's not that big businesses don't have payment problems too, but they have the capital to weather such storms while a small business does not.

The first step

A letter can be the most efficient way of getting a response from many late payers. But it must be a proper letter, not a badly written, vague plea for payment. Many businesses have standard letters, exactly the same for everyone with exactly the same textbook stilted nineteenth-century phraseology, which they seem to think will actually be read, understood and acted upon by the recipient.

Bad example of standard letter

Dear Sir or Madam

With reference to your order of the 6th September, we respectfully beg to inform you that your account with us is now overdue and we request you to regularise your position and effect payment at your earliest convenience.

Thanking you for your anticipated kind attention in this matter.

Yours faithfully

illegible signature
(*No printed name*)
Dickens and Partners

This kind of letter may seem official, effective and efficient, but it is, in fact, ineffective, inefficient, unclear and lacking relevant essential detail. It gives no invoice number or details of the transaction. Even the signature is unclear, which is at the least discourteous and at worst inefficient. It is not even targeted at anyone in particular, just any old sir or madam.

Anyone receiving this letter would have to do extra work just to find out what the letter is actually referring to and exactly who best to refer the letter within their own organisation. It is much more efficient to have a checklist for details of each payment to chase.

Standard letter checklist

Ask yourself these questions.

1. Who will you write to?
2. Who authorised the order?
3. What is the customer's order number?
4. What is the date of the order?
5. What goods or service are we talking about?
6. What is the amount or description of the goods or services?
7. What was the date and place of delivery?
8. Do you have copies of a dispatch note and a goods received note?
9. What is your invoice number and details?
10. Where and to whom did you send the invoice?

This checklist is not set in concrete, i.e. all the details may not be available in every case, but it is a useful guide. Numbers 1, 2, 3, 9 and 10 are usually essential for generating effective action.

Good example of standard letter

Dear Fred/Mary/Mr Jenkins/Mrs Jones etc.

I would be very grateful if you could arrange a cheque for three overdue payments.

The payments concerned are:
1   Invoice No. 67 for a total of £235 (£200 + £ £35 VAT).
Your order number: 8765G/94

2   Invoice No. 68 for a total of £1175 (£1000 + £175 VAT).
Your order number: 8777G/94
3   Invoice No. 79 for a total of £6580 (£5600 + £980 VAT).
Your order number: 8799G/94

As you will see, all these payments are now more than a month overdue.
If there are any problems, please ring or fax me.

Yours sincerely

Your signature
Your name typed
Your phone number
Your fax number

You should have this letter ready to be word processed for each late payment and vary the style of address, using first names only if you really know well or frequently deal with the other person.

Suggested second letter

Dear Fred/Mary/Mr Jenkins/Mrs Jones etc.

We have had no reply to our letter of (*give date of first letter*) about overdue payment(s) on our invoice/invoices (*give invoice numbers or numbers plus amounts and any other relevant details*). This/these payment/s is/are now (*number*) days overdue.

If there is any problem with this/these invoice/s please let us know. If there is no problem we shall expect payment within one week of the date of this letter.

Yours sincerely

Your signature
Your name, typed
Your phone number
Your fax number

Still no action?

Suggested third letter

Dear Fred/Mary/Mr Jenkins/Mrs Jones etc.

We have written to you twice on (*give dates of previous two letters*) regarding the following overdue payment/s. (*Give details of invoice*s and amount*s*).

We are very concerned that our normal credit terms have now been exceeded and we will be ringing you later this week to discuss this.

Obviously, in the circumstances, we cannot accept any more orders for work from you until this/these/ payment/s is/are made. This is our third letter about this matter and we do hope we shall not be forced to take stronger action.

Yours sincerely

Your signature
Your name typed
Your phone number
Your fax number

Four ways to deal with really late payers

1. Phone calls to the accounts department.
2. Letter to the CEO or managing director by name.
3. Personal visit.
4. Fiendish fax or faxual harassment.

Phone calls to the accounts department

Remember: preparation = paperwork + invoice number.

It is never any use at all to ring up an accounts department, and expect them correctly and accurately to translate your worries about your invoice into action if you don't have the detailed paperwork at your fingertips.

Always have the relevant information in front of you. See the Standard Letter Checklist and compile the relevant information, so you are able to find the right person to talk to and answer questions immediately.

Don't say: 'What's the problem with this payment?' This offers a lot of scope for wriggling out of giving any useful answer for the person at the other end of the phone. 'Our computer went down. We've had a lot of problems with software ... etc.' is an old favourite here.

Do say: 'Is there a problem with this payment?' This requires a yes, no or don't know answer, and you are moving closer to a solution, whichever of those you get. If it's 'don't know', you can either hang on while they find out or say you'll ring back for a yes or no in half an hour. This keeps the pressure up and doesn't let them off your hook.

If they agree that there is no problem, suggest a date when they will make the payment. If they say they only make payments on Thursdays, then pin them down to the next Thursday and tell them you expect the cheque to arrive, or the notice that the money has gone directly into the bank, on the following Friday.

Get the name of the person you are talking to: if they think you don't know who they are, they won't bother to give your problem any priority. But if they think you know who they are and will ring them back, they may act to solve your problem a bit sharpish, just to get you out of their hair.

Summarise the points agreed: you can say something like: 'So, Mrs Soap, we've agreed that I will send you one of the invoices again and resubmit that one with the incorrect VAT, and they'll be in the post today. So you'll get them tomorrow, and you can raise a cheque to cover them and post it to me tomorrow afternoon, and then everything will be settled.'

Be prepared to negotiate: on a big debt, it can be foolish to insist on payment in full immediately in every case – even £1000 out of a £5000 debt is a great deal better than the nothing you have at present. If you can get £2000, even better.

If you negotiate and leave the debtor feeling they've retrieved something out of a difficult situation, they will be more willing to pay up than if they feel they've been treated like a naughty schoolchild.

Be careful: someone may ring you unexpectedly and offer a deal which is more advantageous to them than to you. They are trying to surprise you into agreeing to give something up.

Take it slowly: it's always best to be non-committal in these circumstances. Get clear exactly what they're offering, make a note of it and then say you'll ring them back. This takes the initiative away from them and gives it to you. It also gives you time to assess their offer and ring back with everything clear in your mind.

Letter to the CEO or managing director by name

The purpose of any action you take to recover debts is to get a reaction at the other end and ginger up the debtor organisation into making the effort to send you your money. It's a matter of judgement whether your letter to a CEO or a managing director will do any good at all in a large organisation where a trip to the accounts department by one of the high ups is about as frequent as a royal visit. On the other hand, a memo from the top saying 'Action this payment a.s.a.p.' and signed by the MD has been known to shift things when all else has failed.

Getting money owed by large organisations

In 1993 a letter drawn up by the Prince's Youth Business Trust for its young entrepreneurs to try to help them recover money owed by large companies or organisations received publicity in the national newspapers, because it was claimed it worked in three out of five cases of non-payers where it was sent to the CEO of a large organisation with a reputation to preserve.

You can use this letter as a model and work out your own version taking out the reference to the Prince's Youth Business Trust (or young people!) if they are not relevant to you.

Dear (*insert name*)

I write to explain the difficulty in which your highly reputed firm is unwittingly placing me.

As a successful businessman/woman yourself, you will no doubt remember your own early days. I am a very small one man/ woman business set up with help from the Prince's Youth Business Trust and, as you will understand, that organisation only helps those who really need the money to get going. Before they would consider me, I had to draw up a business plan, but it simply didn't allow for reputable firms like yours taking so long to pay. While my terms are payment within XX days of the job being completed/goods being delivered, I have now waited [*insert number*] weeks for payment.

Would you, I wonder, look into this matter for me and arrange in my particular circumstances for a cheque to be sent to me immediately – if only to save my business from becoming another statistic. I would be so grateful to you. I feel sure that it is not the intention of someone like you to stifle entrepreneurial enterprise by making it impossible for young people to trade with successful businesses like yours.

Yours sincerely

Your name
Your job title

The personal visit

A visit in person by you or someone else who works for you can often produce a cheque from a late payer, but it isn't a good idea to go looking for trouble. It can be useful to tie in the collection of a cheque with a meeting you are having anyway to discuss further business. This means you can suggest you collect the cheque when you meet: 'I'm just ringing to confirm our meeting on Tuesday and I've just noticed that your payment for your last order is now overdue. But that's no problem, I can pick up the cheque when I see you – OK?' An approach like this is not hostile and can usefully embarrass the customer into paying up.

If you arrange a meeting only to talk about debts, you must have all the relevant facts at your fingertips, and take copies and photocopies of paperwork with you. You should normally only be in this position if the debt situation is getting very serious, or if there is an unresolved query or complaint by the customer about the order.

Once you are in such a meeting you should be firm and persistent, and prepared to negotiate if necessary. Always take notes of what the other person says and show that you are listening to them – but, on the other hand, put your point of view firmly and carefully. Confrontational stuff like 'I'm not leaving this office without a cheque' is not the best way to proceed: the customer can just call your bluff, walk out and leave you looking stupid.

The best solution is to get what you are owed, or to negotiate a deal either on the amount or on the timing of payments. For instance, it's far better to walk out with a cheque for part of the amount owed plus a post-dated cheque for the rest, than to get nothing at all.

Women are better at debt collecting than men. A year ago I was chasing a man who owed me money, and I got his wife on the phone and she was very sympathetic. She was a debt collector herself and she gave me some very valuable tips. The best one is that men hate to lose face in front of women. So, if you have to go and see a man about a debt, you've got a much better chance of getting money out of him if you're a woman. I've found this really does work and I've used this advice myself by going to see people and politely asking for the money. So the advice is – if you're a woman go and collect the money yourself, and if you're a man, send a woman to do the job.

Barbara Kidd, managing director, Herforder UK Limited

The fiendish fax or faxual harassment

This is definitely not recommended in the majority of cases, but if you really feel you have tried everything else and you have nothing to lose, some people recommend getting a long roll of fax paper or using a large number of sheets of A4 and writing your message spaced out with one word per A4 sheet (or equivalent spacing on the sheet of fax paper) in large letters with a black marker pen. You then feed this special message into your fax machine and send it to your debtor.

A normal first page followed by: 'You owe me £470 (£400 + £70 VAT) — my Invoice Number 102, dated 3 January – ordered by Jane Soap 23 December Order Number 567890/H94. It is now July. This is the first message – others will follow' looks like a pretty brief message in normal circumstances. But it takes up 33 pages of their fax paper at the other end using the fiendish fax method. And most modern faxes are now so clever they won't let a mere human switching them off prevent them from delivering a message. Your fax will be redialling and redialling until it delivers your special fiendish fax, and it will automatically deliver the message as long as the receiving fax is switched on. Most offices need their fax machines switched on, not off, so this technique can cause quite a bit of bother.

Is this faxual harrassment? It has been known to work – fast – but it may be advisable to use it only if you really don't mind tying up your own fax machine and also you really don't care whether or not you get any further business from that client!

Worst-case scenarios

It can be that, despite all your best efforts, you fail to extract the money due to you from a debtor, so what do you do then? There are various last resort options open to you.

Debt collecting agencies

If all else fails and your debt is big enough you may have to consider using a debt collection agency to recover money owing to you.

Debt collection agencies can ease the burden on a business too pressed for time to pursue its debts thoroughly. However, as with factoring (see below), if you use a debt collection agency, you must be prepared to give up a percentage of the amount of the debt recovered to those who have collected it. The advantages of using an agency are that its employees are used to dealing with debts and debtors every day. They know the business and legal procedures involved, and can pursue them quickly and effectively as possible on your behalf. They can advise you whether or not to take action through the County Court or Small Claims Court (see section on Small Claims Courts below), but you should also inform and consult your solicitor and your accountant about this type of procedure. The disadvantages are that the agency has to take its cut, which for smaller debts may not be very cost-effective. As with many other business decisions, the best advice is to ask someone you can trust and who has used a debt collecting agency, about their experience. It's very important to be discreet about bad debts because you only need a word in the wrong ear and suddenly there's a rumour that your business is rocky because you're owed a lot of money!

Here are the questions to ask your expert advisors when all informal approaches have failed.

- Should you issue a statutory demand to the debtor – pay up within 21 days?
- Should you get a court order authorising a sheriff or bailiffs to seize goods to the value of the debts?
- Should you apply for the offending company to be wound up – start liquidation or bankruptcy proceedings?
- Should you try recovery through issuing a writ?
- Should you use the County Court or the Small Claims Court?
- If you have supplied goods, do you still have legal title and, if so, can you get all or some of them back?
- Above all – does the debtor have the funds to pay your debt or any part of it? There is no point spending money going to law if the debtor has nothing at all. This is just throwing good money – your money – away.

Factoring

This involves a specialist company taking over all your debts and recovering all of them for a percentage fee. It is undoubtedly useful for large and medium-sized companies, and the number of factoring firms has grown rapidly in the last decade. For small firms it is a matter of judgement, depending on how many debts you have and how much it is costing you anyway in time taken to recover them or if you can't keep up with your paperwork and are having to write off hard-earned money as bad debts.

WHERE TO GET FINANCIAL AND LEGAL ADVICE

Solicitors

You can get advice free for the first half-hour you see a solicitor to discuss your case. After that, if they take on the case, you have to pay.

Citizens' Advice Bureaux

Some Citizens' Advice Bureaux have solicitors available to give legal advice free of charge on certain days.

Law centres

Lawyers in law centres are aiming at providing legal advice at a price ordinary people can afford and they use Legal Aid wherever they can. They can be useful in being willing to take on test cases to try to prove a point.

Small Claims Courts

Bad debts and other business disputes need not land the small business with a large legal bill. If the amount in dispute is £1000 or less, then the matter can be dealt with in the Small Claims Court. Disputes involving debts, goods not supplies, faulty goods, bad workmanship, accidents and loans can all be taken to the Small Claims Court. The cost to the person bringing the action is low in comparison with other courts and depends on the amount of money being claimed.

The advantages of using the Small Claims Courts, which are based at every County Court, is that they are cheap because lawyers aren't usually retained and the matter should be dealt with quickly. The court will give you the forms needed to begin the action and court staff will tell you what to do next. Citizens' Advice Bureaux can help with filling in forms and procedural advice.

7

Marketing and Selling

■

It's just called 'The Bible' now – we dropped the word 'Holy' to give it more mass-market appeal.

Judith Young, of publishers Hodder & Stoughton, talking in 1989 about a new edition of the world's best-selling book

THE MARKETING PROCESS

HOW YOU SELL your products or services can make the difference between profit and loss – and also the difference between small profits and big profits, or small losses and big losses. Everyone needs some marketing – whether it's formalised and becomes a marketing department as in a large company – or if it's only 'word of mouth' and getting talked about and known by the right people if you're a freelance working alone. Marketing, at its most sophisticated, starts with market research and analysis; it is then concerned with product development based on the research findings; and, finally, all this is followed by pricing, sales and promotion.

Your marketing plans when you're working for yourself do not have to be the most complicated of exercises. You can do your own market research, write your own market research report, then use the guidelines in this chapter to sort out your own marketing, develop your product or service in line with your market assessment, and devise your pricing, sales and promotion plans.

Marketing should be a fundamental part of your business

planning right from the start. It is not an add-on activity – you should think of it as a necessity, never a luxury.

What is the marketing process?

Marketing comes before selling, promotion and advertising. The phrase 'marketing strategy' is commonly used because that's what marketing is – an essential strategy to help you in your business.

Marketing and selling are *not* one and the same thing, so it's important to know the difference between them:

- **marketing** is concerned with ensuring that you provide what customers want to buy;
- **selling** is concerned with getting orders and ensuring that customers buy what you provide.

The simplest definition of marketing is to make what you can sell, instead of trying to sell what you can make.

Your own marketing strategy

You should always have a marketing strategy and know what's going on. Remarkable numbers of people working for themselves don't know what their marketing strategy is, so they make mistakes in approaches to customers – even setting and giving them the wrong prices.

Everyone's busy when they're self-employed – or they should be most of the time – but it's never an excuse for giving customers out-of-date information or, worse, crossing lines with a colleague who has developed a new marketing strategy without telling you or anyone else.

Too much uncoordinated marketing can be as bad as too little. It's the marketing consultant's recurring nightmare to meet those small business people who come in to them for help and say: 'We did some marketing once but it didn't work'.

10 steps to success

1. Assess your market

At its simplest market research means assessing:

- the existing market and its history;
- the likely attitude of customers or potential customers to a present marketing situation;
- the likely attitude of customers or potential customers to a future marketing situation;
- your competitors, their strengths and weaknesses;
- gaps in the market.

2. Make product changes

Don't make changes on a whim or an uninformed hunch. Basing your decision on your market research:

- change your product or service to fit the demand shown;
- create a new product or service to fit the demand shown;
- give the customers what they want.

3. Make a sales forecast

Based on your market research:

- use your judgement to decide what sales are possible or likely;
- analyse your sales forecast in terms of sales per week/per month/per year.

4. Product management

Based on your market research decide these questions:

- What will customers want to buy?
- What quantities will they buy?
- How will this affect your profits?

5. Pricing

Based on your market research and assessment of the competition think about the following:

- What prices should you set?
- What's the best price you can get?
- What discounts should you offer?
  (For advice on pricing see later in this chapter.)

6. Distribution and delivery

- How will you organise distribution of your goods or services?
- How will your customers get delivery of what they've paid for?

7. Sales management

Based on your market research and assessment of the competition:

- plan your marketing to achieve the desired level of sales;
- decide if you need staff – full-time/part-time/temporary;
- decide what equipment and facilities any staff need.

8. Sales promotion

Plan your sales promotion:

- advertising;
- direct marketing;
- public relations;
- your response and follow-up to all your methods of sales promotion.

9. Your sales and marketing plan

- draw up a plan for your sales and marketing effort;
- draw up a budget for your sales and marketing effort.

10. Go for it!

Go for it right where you are

In the Bible there is a saying that you can't make bricks without straw – which has come to mean a general statement about having to have the right ingredients before you do anything. But if you wait that long in your own business you may be waiting a long time. You can either go ahead and make the bricks with what you have to hand, or you can make something different, like pottery, or a mud facepack or a new garden. Be flexible. Be constructive.

Remember another old Jewish saying: 'If life gives you lemons, make lemonade'.

MARKETING METHODS

Selling outlets

You can sell at home, your customer's home, the customer's office, the customer's workshop or factory. If you want advice on selling techniques there are plenty of books with systems and psychological techniques you can read – see the Booklist at the end of this book for more details.

You can also sell in shops, on market stalls, in the street or by mail order, and at trade fairs, conferences or seminars. You can speak at presentations at trade fairs or exhibitions and you are marketing yourself while you speak. If you're good, you won't remember faces from the audience, but they'll remember you, and ring up and ask for you by name.

For some services or products trade fairs can be very valuable in keeping you in touch with rivals and finding out about other businesses, how they do things and new developments.

Contacts and networking

Who you know is always more important than what you know. True or false? Ask most business people, in small or large businesses, and most of them will tell you that in business, knowing people or being known to them through other people, does put you ahead of someone with no connections at all.

Try asking yourself: given a job that needs doing and given two people with apparently equal talents and track records, one of whom you know or have worked with before who has never let you down, and the other you know nothing about, which would *you* choose? The one you know or the one you don't?

But it's useful to take note of that phrase – who has never let you down – because a contact gives you a chance, but only one chance. If you let someone down and don't deliver what they want, when they want, you'll find the door that was opened once will almost certainly be firmly closed the next time you knock on it.

How do you make contacts? You start with the people you already know. And you ask them if they know people who could be useful to you. You make sure you keep their numbers – have a system for writing numbers down and for keeping business cards. Make yourself do this whether you invest in a special plastic book with holders for cards or simply clip cards into a book. And always have you own business cards with you, ready to give out to potential customers.

Business cards, letterheads and leaflets

Normal standards of professionalism in all walks of life now mean that business cards are not just useful but essential. Fortunately, printing is a lot easier than it used to be – faster and more accessible. And with photocopying and desktop publishing you can even provide your own supplies of professional looking stationery.

One of the things you can do at the start is to get your marketing right and get cards and leaflets printed professionally. Never let your customers or clients see you in an unprofessional light.

Targeting and mail shots

Mailings can be a useful marketing tool, but they too need to be targeted. If you have a mailing list, do you know if your mailing list is active, or is it full of names of people who are never going to buy your product or service and who simply file your efforts in the bin?

If you have a computerised mailing system, you can mail a lot of people far quicker than doing the letters one by one and addressing the envelopes by hand. If you need mailings to keep your business alive, you should consider buying some software to enable you to sort out your mailings on your computer. If you haven't got a computer, can you really afford not to have one?

'We often use direct mail and brochures,' says Barbara Kidd, MD of Herforder UK Limited, sole UK agent for a German carpet and flooring company. 'Recently, we produced a survey on flooring needs which we asked people to fill in, telling them that their reward for spending time on this was a free compact disc of their choice. This produced a much higher response than a normal mailing.

'We selected particular architectural practices from the Royal Institute of British Architects yearbook, then targeted one person in each practice, after ringing up to find out who's responsible for ordering flooring. Architects are bombarded with information these days and it's very difficult to get their attention, but this survey was very successful. Our agents went out and bought the CDs and delivered them personally, and used the opportunity to talk about our business. Also, we have the goodwill in the future every time they play the CD.

'For most mail shots the normal percentage of business is about 4–5 per cent – on this one we got 20 per cent. The whole thing cost only about £1500, and you can easily spend that on one ad.'

PRICING

Child: 'What's two plus two?'
Lord Grade, famous film and television entrepreneur:
'Are you buying or selling?'

Quoted in the *Sun*, 22 December 1987

You can't negotiate effectively without knowing your bottom line. That is, you can't work out realistic prices for your products or services unless you have some idea of the lowest amount you can charge to cover your costs and make a small profit – your bottom line below which you cannot afford to fall. And you can't just guess your costs: instinct and trained instinct have their uses in running any business, but guesswork is not useful as a habitual business method.

Your real running costs do not just include the obvious like rents, rates, electricity, equipment, salaries and fees – they also include things like billable and non-billable hours. For instance, if you charge someone strictly by the hour or the day for a job you do for them, are you also charging them for all the time you spent on their behalf? Use the pricing list guidelines to calculate the time you are really spending on a project.

Pricing guidelines list:
- phone calls – cost and time spent;
- meetings – dates and time spent;
- travelling to meetings – costs and time;
- stationery;
- postage;
- hospitality;
- research – cost and time spent;
- planning – time spent;
- follow-up – time spent;
- administration – time spent;
- anything else?

You may be surprised when you work out how much time and resources a particular deal is taking up. At first, you may find it unrealistic to bill clients for everything you have done for them and as you become more experienced you may not take so long on another similar project. Nevertheless, you will have to decide which of your hours are billable and which non-billable – and what sort of rate you are going to settle on to marry up your prices with current market rates.

Some lawyers and accountants start the clock the moment you ring them, and charge you even more if they have to ring or write to you. Are you sure you are building in the right costs and profits to your prices, right from the day you start trading?

'You have to price things right because if you don't it can affect your whole business,' says Pauline Davies of Aunties. 'There are so many hidden expenses in business. You can easily forget the extra time you've spent setting something up, the phone calls, the stationery, the electricity, the petrol or fares, delivery costs etc. A good formula is to work out your basic costs and then double the amount to get your price.

> *It's an easy trap for new businesses to fall into, thinking that your competitors are charging what seem to be high prices just for the hell of it. But you need to work everything out carefully. They may be looking at all the costs, whereas you only see a few of them. They may have it right in general terms, so it's a good idea not to think that undercutting on price is always the only way to get business. People don't always buy on price – they want quality.*

Getting it right

Getting your prices right is one of the trickiest and most demanding tasks when working for yourself. Many freelances regard cheapness as essential to success in generating sales and profits, but low prices are sometimes a trap, not a trading advantage. It is not automatically true that setting your prices low will win you markets. Customers don't always want only the cheapest, they also want the best value for their money.

In fact they may associate cheapness with lack of quality. If they pay more, they may believe they will get better quality. They may think something is too cheap to be worth buying. They may think prices are so low that there must be a catch – probably they will think your products won't last or the service won't be as good as others which cost more. So, in some cases, low prices can put potential customers off.

Cheap prices can make unhappy customers

It's unwise to pay too much, but it's unwise to pay too little. When you pay too much you lose a little money, that is all. When you pay too little, you sometimes lose everything, because the thing you bought was incapable of doing the thing you bought it to do. The common law of business practice prohibits paying a little and getting a lot. It can't be done. If you deal with the lowest bidder, it's well to add something for the risk you run. And if you do that, you will have enough to pay for something better.

John Ruskin, Victorian socialist writer and lecturer on art, architecture, politics and economics, after whom Ruskin College, Oxford, is named

Low prices may have their uses at the start when you want to get going and get some cash flow, but they may be a serious hindrance in the future when your overheads have risen and your prices haven't.

Your aim at the start should be not to set your prices too low. If your prices are too high you can bring them down. It's far harder to be forced to put them up when your customers may only be attached to you because of your low prices.

Obviously, if you are in a business selling one stately home a month and making a big profit on each big sale, you'll have a completely different pricing policy to someone in a business selling millions of baked beans every day of the year and making a tiny profit on lots of sales. Similarly, if your work is very labour-intensive, it may not be much good increasing the volume of sales if you have to take on more people to do the work and therefore cannot make as much profit on more sales as you do on a smaller sales volume.

Sometimes you may have to take the tough decision that you are going to have to stop making one particular product or offering a particular service, even though you may enjoy the work and your customers are happy, because what you are doing is simply not cost-effective. You need to plan carefully, weighing up a number of differing variables when you set prices – and if you do your research well and use your informed judgement, you should be able to use price as part of your strategy both to build your business and to defend it. You may not get your prices right from the start but this doesn't matter so long as your are alert and change your prices in line with your increasing information about your market as you go on trading.

Using price as a weapon

Your long-term decisions on pricing should be aimed at producing the best combination of sales volume, price and costs, as well as making sure your prices conform with your overall image. There are a number of different tactics which can be very useful, whether or not your are using price as a weapon to increase your market at the expense of your competitors. Plan these tactics carefully, then write down your plans and assess them thoroughly before putting them into action.

Short-term price reductions to increase sales

This is lowering your prices to increase sales volume and build business. You may reduce your prices across the board, or you may offer discounts or special offers on specific prices. You may do this to increase profits or you may reduce your profits in the short-term to increase clients and build the business in the long term.

Differential pricing

This is using different prices for different target markets. For instance, you may run a hairdressing service from home and offer cheaper haircuts to pensioners; or you may publicise your business via a newsletter mailed by a professional or trade organisation and make a special offer of a discount to members who respond by filling in the form in the mailing (which can be a useful mutual deal because it gives you access to a new group of potential customers and gives the body sending out the mailing the opportunity to add value to membership by offering special deals).

Another possibility is to use introductory offers and give anyone who becomes a customer before a certain date a discount on full prices for a year or any length of time you think is practical and profitable.

The key to all these offers is that they must be priced to increase sales volume and profits in areas which are not conflicting with your current customers. Pensioners are a clearly defined group and a hairdresser or a fitness teacher offering cheaper rates to people who can show a pension book or card is not likely to face great opposition from non-pensioners. But if you have sold the same thing at different prices to the same customer groups – people who do not perceive any differences between themselves and the person who is getting the same thing at a cheaper rate – you may build yourself a problem and lose already profitable customers because you have not thought through the full implications of your differential pricing.

Maximising unit profits

You can select a market and target it specifically because you know that customers in that market are willing to pay high prices, and you will be able to achieve a high profit on each sale.

Lowering prices to defeat competitors

Sometimes an existing competitor or a new entrant to your market may be threatening your market share and you decide you have to lower your own prices to make it, at worst, difficult and, at best, impossible for this competitor to grab part of the market. You may have to lower your profits in the short-term to defeat competition in the long-term.

Quality, reliability and reputation

Can you deliver quality and reliability? If your prices are low, does this mean you won't be providing a high quality product or service? For example, if you take a risk and allow a junior person to take charge of an order or a project, and they make a mistake, what's the real cost of that mistake? If it means a lost customer and loss of future orders, was it worth saving money by hiring someone cheap instead of someone experienced?

What's your reputation – your credibility – worth to you in real terms? What's the bottom line in terms of your credibility? Are you never going to let a customer down? If so, what are the steps you need to take to safeguard against problems of quality and reliability? Only you can decide what, in the light of these questions, is the best policy for your business.

Always be prepared to review your prices and see them as a dynamic not a static part of your overall business strategy. You may start off merrily thinking you have the right prices and soon find you have to adjust them up or down. This isn't a sign of failure. But if you don't spot the need for adjustments in your prices, you could very quickly be staring failure right in the face.

So always be flexible and ready for change, and be prepared to keep a constant eye on your prices to help your business to develop. Build your pricing strategy to be part of your marketing strategy.

Flyers

Flyer is one of those American-style words that keeps cropping up in those American children's programmes where the gang of kids has to make some money fast as part of the plot. So they waste no time, and get straight on to their little personal computers and produce what we in Britain still call leaflets, detailing their small business venture, and then they hand these out to all and sundry.

The basic business principle here is correct and, once I'd spotted this, I was struck by how often this comes up as a plot line. But the serious point is that a leaflet – whether you deliver it yourself, or pay to have it put into someone else's mailing or local paper – can reach a lot of potential customers relatively cheaply.

Doing a door drop – at its most basic, merely leaving a business card – can drum up business if you identify your target areas and go for them. This can work for plumbers or taxi drivers for instance, because some people keep the cards in case they ever need the service offered.

Newsletters

You can use your mailing lists to keep in touch with mailings – for example, why not produce and send out a newsletter? You can be the star of your own newsletter even if it's only the absolute minimum of two pages printed back to back. Sending out newsletters does not guarantee that everyone will read them – many will not, but some will, and even those who merely glance at the front page will see that your company is making products or producing services which are 'New' and 'Unique' and 'First'.

You can get experts to write in your newsletter once you can budget for four pages. They do this for nothing, but they get free advertising of their expertise and business to your mailing list, and you get a feature which interests your clients and makes them think you're really someone producing a newsletter with proper features in it. Articles could be about graphology, reflexology, childcare, laptop computers, personal finance, media training etc.

The point of it all is that you and your business are important enough to produce your own newsletter, and you think the former client or potential client is important enough to get it and want to read it. A newsletter can be a very powerful public relations and marketing tool if produced properly. But it does take a lot of work, and you need to allocate enough time to produce it properly.

Advertisements

When they hear the word marketing, a lot of people will immediately start to think of advertising as the most obvious way of marketing any product or service. But advertising, even in a small way, for instance, in local papers, is not always the best or the only way for a small business person to proceed.

Advertisements cost money – a few pounds in local papers, hundreds of pounds in national or regional newspapers, many more hundreds, even thousands of pounds on local radio stations, and many thousands of pounds on local or national television.

The best way to appear in newspapers is frequently in editorial which is free and mentions you and your business in positive terms. Local newspaper ads can be useful for some people, but useless for others. The key factor is working out who your target audience is. Where are these potential customers and what do they read? Companies offering house sitting services – people to look after your house while you're away on holiday – go for glossy magazines with readers who can afford their service. They don't bother with a local free newspaper that goes to every house, including people who can't even afford holidays let alone house sitters.

Setting out advertisements

Advertisements are measured in column inches or column centimetres. You may be offered discounts for more than one booking and you should consider whether it will be more cost-effective to have a series of ads building up customer recognition, rather than just one advertisement which will almost certainly be quickly forgotten.

But never advertise in newspapers just for the sake of it, because you think you should. You might spend two or three hundred pounds on a small ad in a national newspaper, get a handful of replies and not one of them becomes a client because they are not really the people at which your product or service is aimed.

What are you paying for?

You may be asked whether you want to have a border round the edge of the ad, so it looks as though it's in a box. You will be charged more for that than an ad with just text. You pay more the more prominent the page and the position on the page.

People selling ad space for newspapers are all trained salespeople so they will try various selling lines on you to get you to agree to pay for an ad or ads. They almost always say that the space you have decided you want isn't available and then they offer you something more expensive – usually double what you originally specified. They also tell you that you have the last ad available on a particular page – you're very lucky it's still available etc. It's always advisable to say you'll ring them back 'after I've talked over these prices with my colleagues. We're having a meeting tomorrow morning,' you say bravely, trying to slow down the pace and stop them rushing you in to a deal which has now reached twice the budget you had planned.

There is an old adage in advertising – though we don't do any advertising ourselves – that an advert is probably only starting to work for the public when you are sick of it! This applies to most forms of marketing. We do a lot of marketing, but it doesn't matter how much you market your- selves. That's just the peg. It's what you deliver that counts. We market ourselves as women financial advisers who have a distinctive approach, and we have to deliver that.

Fiona Price, Fiona Price and Partners Ltd

Free editorial

There is no doubt that getting free good publicity is the best way of building up your public image both personally and profession- ally. The two go together if you have a small business.

A basic PR campaign

The first thing to realise is that if you're going to try to get some good publicity in newspapers and magazines, and even on local radio or television, you are going to have to talk to journalists. If you find this a distasteful thought, and consider journalists to be generally on the level of something you wipe off your shoe after walking through a stable full of horses, you will either have to change your attitude or find someone else to front your public relations campaign, or just give up the whole idea.

Talking to journalists is not the worst experience anyone could have, but it does mean you will face questioning – sometimes very direct, probing questioning – and not everyone likes or can get used to that. Other people take to it like a duck to water, and sail off getting more and more and better and better newspaper cover- age, to the envy of their rivals and competitors.

However you feel about being questioned, it does no harm to practise. You should get used to people asking you straight ques- tions and expecting direct replies. Listen to the local radio, watch local television programmes and put yourself in the position of some of the interviewees. If you're going to hold a press conference, get a colleague, friend or family member to ask you searching questions.

Free publicity – editorial in papers, sound on radio, and sound and vision on television – does have a cost. It costs your time and if you feel that your time could be better spent than in talking to journalists, you would be well advised not to start talking to journalists at all, because journalists know when people don't want to talk to them and it's not exactly going to get them on your side, is it?

If you want publicity you must take it seriously – be prepared to give up your time, both in devising press releases and events to raise media interest, and in responding to that interest if it is aroused.

Press releases

Guidelines

- Always print a press release on headed paper.
- Always use double spacing.
- Make sure your phone number is prominent on both the front page and the second page.
- If possible, keep to one or two pages.
- Date the press release at the end.
- Put a headline at the top – centred above the first paragraph.
- Make your main point in the first paragraph.
- Make it clear who is saying what and make it interesting.
- Avoid jargon – and if it is used, explain it.
- Put 'Jane Soapsud is available for interview on Thursday after the press conference.' It's quite normal for TV and radio reporters to want to interview you *before* the press conference, so be prepared for that and keep the time available.
- At the end of the press release put: for further information, contact Jeff Bubble, Press and Public Relations Officer (*or whoever*), Telephone . . . Fax number . . . Home number . . .

I know you'll find this hard to believe but every day press releases are posted or faxed to journalists without names or contact numbers on them. There are many unprofessional press releases about, so don't be afraid of having a go yourself, following the guidelines I've given and always giving clear information, clearly set out and clearly written.

The example of Jane Smith on page 200 is geared to a local paper and it gives them everything they need – including time of next event, quotes, a bit of background, further information – one page only – and the fact that a photo is available.

You might decide to send out the photo with the press release. If you do, you must type a caption and stick it on the back. But you could be wasting your hard-earned money as newspapers get sent lots of photos and don't treat them with much respect, putting many of them straight in the bin. The availability of the photo is in fact a tease to get someone to ring you and ask for it.

Here is some advice:

- send the press release two weeks before the event;
- always follow up by ringing the newsdesk to ask them if they're interested;
- if they are keen find out if they are part of a chain of local newspapers and whether you'll be used in more than one paper;
- if your story is used, be prepared for it to be picked up by the local radio station and decide whether you want to be interviewed and what you want to say. You won't usually get a lot of notice of a radio interview – often the same day or next day – so being ready for it is an advantage.

The second example of John Jones's press release is to publicise something outside work and not related to it, but something which gives the opportunity for publicity.

Note that both press releases have the magic words 'new' and 'first' in the first paragraph. Journalists will assess for themselves exactly how new or first your efforts are, but at least it gives them a reason to read your release, while many others fail at the first hurdle by creating no interest at all in the journalist reading them.

How to talk to the press and broadcast media

If you're going to start trying to use the press and broadcast media to promote yourself and your products or services, you need to know what you are letting yourself in for – before you start. *The first and most important rule for talking to journalists is if you don't want them to know something –don't say it.*

JANE SMITH, AROMATHERAPIST

PRESS RELEASE   *For immediate release*

AROMA PARTIES IN HIGH WYCOMBE

Aromatherapist Jane Smith has dreamed up a new way of relaxing and keeping her customers happy – she's organising aroma parties every month at her home in High Wycombe. The parties are from 6.30 p.m. to 8.30 p.m. every first Wednesday in the month, and already Jane has offered a glass of fruit juice and a demonstration of the applications and uses of essential oils, the key to aromatherapy, to more than 40 people in the last 2 months.

   Jane, who is a qualified aromatherapist and aromatherapy teacher, says the parties are so popular because they provide a relaxing social occasion with a difference. 'Some people have told me they love coming to my "smelly parties"' and Jane stresses the parties are alcohol free and no rival to the infamous parties and orgies of High Wycombe in the eighteenth century. 'But I'm sure some of the young Regency dandies would have liked to try aromatherapy as well as all the other things they got up to, if it had been around in their time' she adds.

   The next party is on 8 February.

For further information – contact Jane Smith
Daytime 01123 456567   Fax 01123 456578
Evening 01123 234354

A photo of Jane Smith is available if required. Further information about Jane is attached.

JOHN JONES, BUILDER AND DECORATOR

PRESS RELEASE   *For immediate release*

ROOFER TAKES THE PLUNGE

Gateshead builder, John Jones, will be making the biggest jump of his life on Saturday 29 March when he climbs up the Tyne Bridge to make a bungee jump for charity.

This is the first time any jumps have been authorised from the Tyne Bridge and John, 44, will be one of only four people allowed to make the jump. He has never made a bungee jump before but wants to make the effort because his wife works for Oxfam and he wants to raise money for their Africa Appeal. 'It'll be the biggest jump of my life' he says, 'and although I've been a roofer for 30 years and I've a good head for heights I'm not used to jumping off when I'm high up. But my customers needn't worry. I won't be practising by leaping off their roofs.'

PHOTOCALL
Date: Saturday 29 March.
Time: 11.00 a.m. for jump at 11.45 a.m.
Rendezvous: Tyne Bridge Lifts, Quay Street, Newcastle upon Tyne

For further information – contact John Jones
Daytime 01123 456567   Fax 01123 456578
Evening 01123 234354

A photo of John Jones is available if required. Further information about John is attached.

1. Don't try to be clever and talk about things being 'unattributable' or 'off the record'. You are not a politician or a member of the royal family, and journalists may simply not take the trouble to remember whether you said something and then said 'Don't quote me – that was off the record'. Journalists are paid to spot embarrassing points and if you say something you shouldn't to a radio or television interviewer, they'll almost certainly remember and ask you about it in a live interview.

2. Try not to score points by badmouthing a particular competitor. The kind of thing you say to your friends about rivals or competitors may be 'great copy' for a journalist, but could backfire in print or on radio or TV and at worst you could find yourself at the end of a writ if a competitor thinks they can make a case against you. Far better to talk in general about how what you offer is far better than other people because . . .

3. Prepare your points before you get on the phone to any journalist – preferably ask a friend not in your line of business what sort of questions they would ask you. When you're close to a subject it's almost inevitable you will ignore the obvious, and get tripped up and your credibility undermined by a perfectly fair question which you should know the answer to, but haven't got the information to hand. For instance: 'How many other people offer a gardening service like yours in this area?' You need to know whether it's 0, 2, 3, or 25, and exactly what makes you different from the rest.

4. Always prepare yourself for any media interview by deciding what points you want to make and what information you want to use to back them up. When you're doing an interview don't try to branch off into an area you haven't prepared. If you haven't got the right facts you'll be caught out and again your credibility will suffer.

5. Keep a cuttings file and record any radio or television interviews. Use the cuttings as part of your marketing to get more work in the future. Use the broadcast interviews as training for yourself. Work out what went well and what didn't, and learn for the next time. In addition watch the TV and listen to the radio carefully, and analyse other people's interviews. If you think you're going to need to use broadcast media interviews a lot to publicise yourself and your services, investigate getting some media training. One day's training can be a very worthwhile investment and save you from embarrassment, because doing broadcast interviews is not as easy as it looks when you see the finished products on news bulletins and other programmes.

IMPORTS AND EXPORTS

Always do your basic detailed research before you start importing or exporting, both in the UK and abroad. This is not an area for buskers – you need to have a detailed grasp of regulations at both ends of your deals. Market research is essential.

For instance, when you are importing, the legal responsibility to ensure that relevant taxes and importation charges are assessed and paid rests solely with the importer. Contact your local Customs and Excise to find out the correct commodity code and what charges are applicable.

Contact the Department of Trade and Industry's Import Licensing Branch to find out if there are any restrictions, prohibitions or special licences required for the product you want to import, and what the procedures are for applying for that licence.

Surveys by the Institute of Export show that too many small firms wishing to export are insular in their approach. They face difficulties because they do not do their homework thoroughly. They will sell only in sterling because they have no strategy for handling foreign exchange.

Exporting can be extremely profitable and strengthen a small business, but it can also stretch and strain the existing financial and marketing skills of small companies. Many fear it will over-stretch them and they ignore the possibilities of exporting because they believe it is too complicated and will put too much pressure on them.

Before exporting you should conduct extensive market research to identify:

- which country has a suitable market for your product;
- what the legal requirements and technical standards are for your product in that country;
- how easy or difficult it is to transport goods there and distribute them.

If you do not feel you want to start exporting directly, there are other opportunities to get your goods sold abroad. Export merchants may specialise in exporting the sort of product you are interested in. They bear all the responsibilities for the exportation and you treat them as though they were domestic customers. Alternatively, you could sell direct to the UK buying houses of overseas companies.

This is a very swift outline of the world of imports and exports. If you want to take it further you should research your market and relevant rules and regulations thoroughly, and contact the Department of Trade and Industry (DTI), the Institute of Export, and the Association of British Chambers of Commerce. The DTI basic booklet, 'How To Start Exporting', is particularly useful. See Checklist 3 on importing and exporting at the end of this book.

TENDERING FOR GOVERNMENT CONTRACTS

Until only a few years ago government contracts were far less open to tender than they are now and they were mainly the preserve of large companies. Small organisations just weren't thought of as being on the same planet as civil servants making massive contract decisions for large numbers of huge government departments.

Public bodies spend billions of pounds each year on goods and services, and they are always looking for new suppliers. The public sector includes central government, local government, the National Health Service, and schools, universities and colleges. All these organisations are now encouraged to cut out waste and get value for money for the public.

All kinds of supplies from pencils to toilet rolls, to curtains, to stationery, to secretarial training, to making videos, to paint, paintbrushes and electrical plugs, are needed. It all has to come from somewhere and, increasingly, civil servants are being urged to look at what small business people have to offer.

Get on the approved tenderers list

In order to be eligible for doing business with the government you need to be accepted on to a list of potential suppliers. Officials have to ask for a minimum of three tenders for contracts and they need lists of people they can invite to tender for contracts.

Getting on a list is not always easy. It's necessary to be persistent, and find out exactly what information people want and then give it to them. Getting on to a list may not be permanent as lists can be reviewed and names removed.

The DTI produces a useful free booklet called 'Tendering for Government Contracts' specifically aimed at small businesses, and packed with information addresses and phone numbers.

Opening up of the public sector market is a significant opportunity for all businesses large and small and, with persistence, it's an opportunity that could benefit many small firms providing a wide variety of products and services.

EIGHT TOP MARKETING TIPS

1. Keep a list of your clients as a marketing tool and value it.
2. Send your client list to prospective new customers or mention existing clients on your CV.
3. Get approving quotations from satisfied customers and use them in your marketing.
4. Know your clients: 'You should think of your customers as partners, or better still, 'family,' according to Victor Kiam, president and chief executive of Remington Products.
5. Remember, the customer is always right. We've all heard of or read this oft-repeated phrase, but not everyone can hear or read, can they? Otherwise those humorous training videos, with comedian John Cleese playing a smug salesman who thought he was right in not having things in stock while the customer was wrong to ask for them, and so on, would never have sold so well, not only in Britain but in Europe and elsewhere in the world of business. Rule two? If the customer is ever wrong, re-read rule one! You need your customers, so never dismiss their criticisms or questions – at least never to their face – unless you think they really are more trouble than they're worth and you can live without them. But still – always be polite. Remember, any customer, even a bad customer, has the power to do you down and damage you in the eyes of other, better, prospects.
6. Give them more than your competitors. 'Do something for his kids. It always means far more to a customer than doing anything for him,' says Mark McCormack, top sports and

entertainment agent and head of International Management Group, which handles many top sports stars.

7. Consider socialising with your customers. There are customers or clients who would run the London Marathon rather than meet business acquaintances socially and others who will enjoy themselves at your expense. Some of the latter will remember you more warmly next time they make a business decision and feel indebted to you. Networking, asking your friends for advice, doing business with friends where appropriate, has its place. Remember, however, that you can ruin a friendship when a business deal isn't quite what your friend anticipated. 'What do you mean, the *Encyclopaedia Britannica* is being delivered? I though I just signed for the free pen!' Imposing your business needs on a friendship may not always be a bright idea.

8. Always look for new customers and try to keep a broad customer base. You have to depend on your customers or clients for your livelihood, but you should always be careful not to be over-dependent on just one or two big sources of income. Too small a customer base can be disastrous. If you commit yourself to one big customer or client, you are taking on their risks. Your business is at risk from anything that damages the company you are depending on. For instance, if they have a serious business problem, such as a fall in demand, a strike, a shortage of their supplies or even an accountant who fiddles their books, you and your business can be badly damaged, even though these problems are nothing to do with you and you can have no influence over them at all.

You may also be vulnerable to staff changes. These can happen very suddenly and you can find that a source of income you are depending on can vanish overnight like melting snow, just because the person who used to commission your services has left, and the new person wants a change or their own contacts they want to use and to boost for their own career purposes. Or maybe there's a new boss who wants to make their name by making a lot of changes, and the easiest people to change are small business people and freelances without fixed long-term contacts.

Whatever kind of service or product you are providing, you need to protect yourself and your business against sudden changes as much as possible.

8

Wealthy and Healthy?

———■———

One of the symptoms of approaching nervous breakdown is the belief that one's work is terribly important. If I were a medical man, I should prescribe a holiday to any patient who considered his work important.

Bertrand Russell, philosopher

COPING WITH STRESS

ALL PEOPLE who are their own bosses face stress. There is almost always too much to do and too little time in which to do it. Demands on your time and energy come from clients, from suppliers, business partners, colleagues or staff, and family and friends. Sometimes all these competing and conflicting demands seem to happen in one day. And the telephone just never stops ringing. And ringing. And ringing. You don't have time to write down one enquiry before there's another and then another.

But, when you're running your own show, you can't afford to get ill. You can't afford to have headaches or be unable to function properly. You need to be able to cope with stress in varying degrees as part of your everyday business life.

For people who have previously been employed by others, the idea that they are suddenly responsible for everything that happens to them while they work can be very stressful – frightening even. Others find it liberating to be free of working directly for others and regard their new business as a liberation. But they can still be stressed by the conflicting demands on their time which working for yourself always brings.

Not all stress is bad. Being keyed up has its place, but you could be living an apparently ordinary life and yet taking risks with your health because of lack of exercise, lack of relaxation and lack of knowledge of how to lead a healthier lifestyle. What you need to watch out for are the signs of stress and you need to know when you are over-stressed.

Avoiding stress

Is your lifestyle dangerous? What, me? Yes, you. You may not be someone who goes bungee-jumping or parachuting or pot-holing, or drives too fast on motorways, but if you have a lot of stress in your life and you don't keep fit, you could be living dangerously despite an 'ordinary' lifestyle.

There's been a lot of discussion in recent years about whether a certain amount of stress is normal and healthy. People vary in the levels of stress they can successfully cope with – one person's 'normal' working day could be another person's route to a nervous breakdown, because it's not the amount of stress, but the stressful effects on you personally, that can cause problems.

When stress is becoming a problem, it involves both mental and physical symptoms, and there are some guidelines which everyone can follow and understand. Most people can work out that a so-called 'ordinary' lifestyle, which includes no physical exercise, lots of smoking and drinking, lots of fatty foods and constant tension during the working day, is far from healthy. You may not be able to get rid of everything making you tense at work, but you can make your diet more healthy, cut down or cut out nicotine and alcohol, and introduce some exercise into your weekly routine.

If you don't put some effort into making this an important part of your schedule, you could be on the road to being at risk from high blood pressure, hypertension and even a heart attack or stroke. The Health Education Council has reported that coronary heart disease remains the leading cause of death in Britain killing more than 150,000 people each year – that's an average of one death every three to four minutes. Men are still twice as likely as women to suffer from coronary heart disease, but the totals for both sexes are still rising in Britain, with heart disease now rising faster among women than men.

Stress-related illnesses, such as hypertension, heart problems, stomach ulcers, lung problems and high blood pressure, are all increasing among women, who are joining men in suffering from these kinds of problems – and losing days at work, usually due to stress.

Recognising the signs of stress

The more extreme symptoms of stress can include difficulty in sleeping, constant tiredness, headaches, indigestion, constipation, breathlessness, sweating, skin diseases and frequent crying or feeling like crying.

And those are just *some* of the physical symptoms. People who are not coping with stress also have mental signs of tension, including constant irritability with themselves and other people, feelings of failure, difficulty in making decisions, fear of the future, loss of interest in other people, fear of disease and difficulty in concentrating. They are also aware that they have angry feelings at the situation they are in and these feelings are suppressed because they feel no one understands them anyway.

Most of us have some or all of these feelings at some time. You don't need to feel you are going slowly round the bend just because you recognise some or all the symptoms of stress outlined above. Everyone can feel very fed up and frustrated at times, but this is not the same as living for months and months, even years and years, with that sort of lifestyle. And if that is your problem, you may not even recognise that you have a problem.

Stress management

One way of coping with stress is to analyse it calmly, but you can't do that while you are stressed.

First of all you need to recognise you are stressed and then try to calm yourself down. Sitting comfortably, straight not slumped, take five deep breaths, counting to ten when you breathe in and counting to ten again when you breathe out. It doesn't sound much, but if you do it properly – which means as slowly as you can – it's very effective. If possible, breathe through your nose, not your mouth.

Follow this with another five deep breaths counting to 15 when you breathe in and out. Make a conscious effort to relax your shoulders and move them down. Roll your head round from shoulder to shoulder very slowly five times. Clench and unclench your fingers, and flex your fingers as though you are playing a piano. Clench and unclench your toes, and feel the tension ease. Keep breathing slowly and gently. Get our of your chair and walk slowly up and down taking deep breaths for at least five minutes.

That's dealing with the symptoms – now tackle the causes.

What's causing your stress?

Are you being too rigid in your attitudes – whether to your work colleagues, children or partners? Are you trying to get everything in your life to fit into set patterns and then becoming stressed when nothing fits? Try to be more flexible. Think of alternatives and use them.

On the other hand, are you too flexible already? Are you frustrated because you're always putting your own interests behind those of others? Can you learn to be more assertive and less willing to fit your life around other people? Can you – whether you're too rigid or too flexible, or somewhere in between the two extremes – recognise the signs of stress?

The key factor leading to stress is lack of control over your life or some parts of it. Since most of the people interviewed for this book emphasised that one of the best things about working for yourself is not having the stress of a boss standing over you, you might assume they would all be unstressed. But, of course, this freedom from the boss means that some of the stress the boss used to cope with now comes crashing straight over you and it can feel like a tidal wave, giving you no time to breathe.

Stress questionnaire

Are you overstressed?

	Yes	No
1. Do you have difficulty in sleeping?	☐	☐
2. Do you have difficulty concentrating?	☐	☐
3. Are you constantly tired?	☐	☐
4. Do you frequently get headaches, indigestion or constipation?	☐	☐
5. Do you ever suffer from breathlessness?	☐	☐
6. Do you ever suffer from sweating?	☐	☐
7. Do you ever suffer from skin diseases?	☐	☐
8. Do you frequently cry or feel like crying?	☐	☐
9. Are you constantly irritable with yourself and other people?	☐	☐
10. Do you have feelings of failure?	☐	☐
11. Is it difficult for you to make decisions?	☐	☐
12. Do you fear the future?	☐	☐
13. Are you worried about catching infectious diseases?	☐	☐
14. Do you care about your colleagues?	☐	☐
15. Do you find these questions really irritating?	☐	☐

If you can answer **yes** to more than half these questions, you should consider whether you are overstressed, and whether you should go and talk to your doctor, and also sort out your work and home environments to cut down on your stress.

I had a boss once in BBC radio who said 'Yes yes yes', or 'Right right right', or 'Good good good', to every suggestion made to him. And you could tell after only a brief acquaintance that absolutely nothing was going in: you could say the same thing again in the afternoon and he would say exactly the same again, and never act on anything because he was much too busy being stressed to do anything else. He made a career out of being stressed – for about a year – then it all become too much and he went on to something quieter.

Stress tips from the frontline

A couple of years ago we went through a very stressful period. On the surface I handled it well, but it was very hard and I've learned to pace myself more and take things more at my own pace. I do go to the gym regularly. I have to have a couple of hours a week away from the children and the business.

Angela Mclean, Rainbow Cleaning Services

I've got a horse, but I never have time to go riding. The business has taken over my life and I find that a change is as good as a rest. So, if I'm in the shop, or cooking the supper or picking flowers, or weeding, it's all different. I love being outside, so any of those jobs are refreshing.

Jacquie Hyde, Field Flowers

To reduce stress, I try to make sure I talk to at least one friend every day. Working on your own can lead you to feel isolated and stressed. I need to do something creative every day, perhaps trying something new or simply coming up with a good idea for a client. I spend a few moments recognising what I am happy about in my life – even when things look grim, there's usually something. I also have a range of techniques, including meditation, for relieving stress and I am blessed with some wonderful friends who practise their own skills on me such as shiatsu massage.

Celia Kemsley, Market Openings

Aromatherapy can be very powerful in helping people to cope with stress. Because it's holistic treatment you are not just treating the symptoms but the whole person. It might be that people are emotionally distraught and you have to deal with their emotions as well as the physical symptoms. It deals with physical, mental and emotional health. It can't just be propaganda – interestingly, animals respond to the oils as well and no one tells them that this is good for them.

Ann Corsie, Reading School of Aromatherapy

I play football twice a week, and go jogging.

Mark Wray, Willy Wiper

I do meditation and I have learned to look after myself, and be aware and keep a balance in my life. I have trained as a healer. I am a radionics practitioner and I use essential oils and Bach flower remedies for healing and for my own health. I also have two cats and a horse.

Fiona Price, Fiona Price and Partners Limited

I have masses of stress. Trying to collect money owed to you definitely raises the blood pressure. I try not to drift into the kitchen and over to the biscuit tin. I play squash and a bit of golf, and I'm very keen on keeping fit because that helps me to keep going. Working from home is a good job for a woman with a family. I have juggled home, two children and an elderly mother, and my husband has helped by being supportive without interfering. When he does interfere, I throw things and shout a lot.

Barbara Kidd, Herforder UK

I think it's not just the amount of work you do, the work environment also plays a big part in your levels of stress. If you're constantly under pressure you will be unhappy and stressed, but we run a happy-go-lucky place where we can laugh and joke and have fun as well as work hard.

I also make sure I have one day off a week and I take the three hours off in the evenings. We also have two two-week holidays a year and get right away from work. The worst, most stressful days are Mondays and Thursdays, the delivery days – but then I find the days without deliveries pretty boring because there isn't so much to do.

I don't want to expand and run another shop. I don't have room to expand here so if I did want to get bigger I'd have to take on another shop and rely on other people more, and that's where the stress comes in. I have a good living here and I don't want the stress of worrying about relying on other people for too much of my income.

Atul Karavadra, Karavadra Supermarket

I wake up every morning with a checklist of things I've got to do. Sometimes I wake up at 2 o'clock in the morning and make lists. But after a run each morning it all falls into place.

Mary Spillane, CMB Image Consultants

Keep a sense of proportion

Remember that today's crisis is usually tomorrow's forgotten detail. As the Arab proverb says: 'The dogs bark, but the caravan passes on.'

ARE YOU FIT FOR BUSINESS?

Physical fitness builds stamina and makes you more able to cope with stress.

Everyone working on their own is under stress and stress without fitness can lead to serious health problems. Stress without fitness can also lead to tired, run-down people without the reserves to cope with long working hours and the pressure of constant decision making.

Not keeping fit could cost you contracts and contacts if you're not on the ball enough to spot openings or stitch ups when they arise. It can also mean you reach the end of your tether sooner than a fitter person, and start shouting and being angry when you should be thinking clearly.

Keeping fit also builds your stamina and without stamina you will find it very hard to get enough done, to keep going that extra mile when you have to, and still get up the next morning and be fresh enough to tackle another set of problems. Keeping fit makes it easier for you to have the stamina to cope with travel if you have to – particularly travel which takes you away from home overnight or abroad.

Keeping fit is not a luxury if you are working on your own or in a small organisation that depends on you. Even if you walk for just 15 minutes twice a day, you will be leaner and fitter than if you sit in the office, or in the car and don't use your legs. If you can take some form of regular exercise whether it's walking, running, swimming, playing tennis, squash or badminton, joining classes for aerobics, yoga or the martial arts, you will feel the benefits every day.

Fitness tips from the frontline

When you're an entrepreneur, you need to look successful. You have to have clear eyes and skin plus energy and vitality. When you walk through a door, the first impression should be of your energy. Fitness gives that to you. If you walk into a room panting and slump into a chair, you're not going to get the order or the contract, or even a day's work. If someone is energetic, they give the impression of more value for money. If someone is lethargic and slow, the impression is they think slower than average and you begin to think you'll be paying them just to breathe. I'm 44 and I'm a fitness fanatic. I run 20 miles a week. I go to a gym and I walk 15 miles at weekends with family. Keeping fit is not a luxury, it's essential. Not just for image consultants but for all entrepreneurs. If you look tired and unfit, you don't look successful and no one's going to listen to your message whatever you're trying to sell them.

Mary Spillane, CMB Image Consultants

I sit around a lot because I'm a writer. Being locked on the keyboard is not good for the brain or the hips so I swim regularly and I go to a stretch workout class twice a week. Going to classes doesn't just keep you fit, it stimulates your mind, and keeps you in touch with the real world and real people. If you work on your own, you really need to make contact with others, to keep your confidence up and to get things in proportion.

Deanna Maclaren, novelist and journalist, author of several romantic novels

I do cycle riding and swimming to keep fit, things I can do with the whole family.

Anna Murphy, AA Music

I seem to go through phases. At the moment I'm really lazy. For the past four years I would ride in Epping Forest once a week, but I found the travelling time out to the forest was more than I could spare, and now I go only occasionally. I sing with two choirs. I sail when I can and I have periods of going out for morning jogs.

Celia Kemsley, Market Openings

I think it's essential to be physically fit. Staying healthy helps you to keep your perspective. Until 1986, I rowed boats internationally, culminating with the Commonwealth

Games in Edinburgh where I rowed for Wales. I ride horses competitively in Sussex where I live.

Fiona Price, Fiona Price and Partners Limited

THE IMPORTANCE OF TIME MANAGEMENT

Keeping fit and keeping your stress levels under control can calm you down and help you to cope with demanding work. Now that you've stopped rushing around under stress, you need to consider whether you are managing your time effectively.

It was Professor C. Northcote Parkinson who, in the 1950s, invented the now legendary popular concept called Parkinson's law. 'Work expands so as to fill the time available for its completion,' he wrote.

'General recognition of this fact,' he continued, 'is shown in the proverbial phrase, "It is the busiest man who has time to spare".' This last phrase has now been modernised to the snappier and less sexist version – 'If you want something done, ask a busy person'.

It was Parkinson's theory that all work, but especially paperwork, is vulnerable to his law, and he used civil servants as his example of a group of people who will always make work for themselves, using frequent memos, reports and meetings to do so.

Beware of home pottering

But the making up of unnecessary tasks is so easy too for anyone running their own business, especially those based at home. Pottering around the kitchen and other rooms in the house, getting your thoughts together, doing a bit of light tidying up, can be allowable for up to 10 or 15 minutes of your own valuable time, but how much is it costing you?

I have a friend who calls pottering about her 'thinking time' and claims that repetitive, non-brain draining household tasks are a kind of soothing mantra to prepare the mind for real brain work. This can be a valid viewpoint if you are being self-aware and aware of how you are using your time, but no use if you are just drifting around putting off doing the quarterly VAT return, or avoiding making that difficult phone call to pitch for a big new order, or just breathing gently while painting or polishing something instead of summoning up extra energy to deal with writing a complicated proposal in a business letter.

But be very careful – this is an extremely slippery slope. For the home-based worker, light tidying up can lead on to the hard stuff, like dusting, hoovering, sorting out the washing, descaling the kettle, looking for that really vital birthday card for Auntie Ivy (which should be in a drawer but isn't), and where are those petrol receipts from last week, and isn't the *Financial Times* interesting this morning – every article is so relevant it must be read right through, mustn't it?

Some people see the dangers and are very strict about not doing any household tasks during their working day. Others exploit the benefits of being at home during the day to complete small tasks or to let in someone to repair the video/washing machine/phone etc. Whatever suits your temperament, you must keep a grip and avoid long-term pottering at home.

Beware of work pottering

I like work; it fascinates me. I can sit and look at it for hours. I love to keep it by me: the idea of getting rid of it nearly breaks my heart.

Jerome K. Jerome in his novel *Three Men in a Boat*

You must also be aware of the great dangers from pottering within your work environment. You can potter wherever you work – you don't have to be working at home to be tempted.

You may sit down at your desk and potter. It is possible to spend a whole morning doing nothing really constructive – by, for instance, doing nothing but filing documents, making nonvital phone calls, rearranging the stationery drawer or cupboard, rearranging files physically in filing cabinets, rearranging files on the computer screen and, worst of all, deciding that now is the time to reprogram all the software on your computer. Clearing out office or workshop cupboards can be a big danger signal here too.

Why is prolonged pottering so dangerous?

Because a potterer is simply waiting for something else to happen. A potterer is not being dynamic, proactive or switched-on. For a short time, this may be useful for recharging batteries, allowing ideas to emerge, reducing stress etc. But no matter how many reasons you can think of to make it useful, it has very limited real benefits.

In fact, if this gets out of hand (probably, for most people, more than an hour of pottering about away from real action!) this is not pottering – useful or otherwise. This is displacement activity, wasting working time while trying to put off getting down to real constructive, often difficult, work.

This is where time management comes in.

What is time management?

Celebrities can be late. Film stars and singers can be later. I recently recorded an interview with the singer Shirley Bassey for a television programme. Thirty minutes after she should have arrived I rang her agent. Yes, she was really definitely coming they said. No, she had not changed her mind. In fact she was only 35 minutes late. Not bad at all really in the star punctuality stakes. And when she did arrive she was very pleasant, and not at all condescending or offensive as some of the Always Very Late Big Stars often are.

But you are not a star – not yet at least – even if you want to be. And lateness is rudeness in business – and, if you are naturally a Late Person, you will have to make a big effort to find a method of dealing with this element of your character.

You can use lateness, but only if you feel you really have the whip hand in a deal. Then lateness and the 'make 'em wait' tactic can be part of a strategy to make people appreciate you more and show them who's boss.

How to manage your time effectively

Is time on your side or always working against you? Do you always feel under pressure with too many things to do and not enough time to do them in? If you have the feeling that time is always slipping away from you and you're never really in control of your work, then you could benefit from looking at the concept of time management.

Some people will not need to read this section in detail: they are born time managers, never later for appointments, always with a well-organised and tidy workspace; they also appear to know instinctively how to delegates tasks to other people. You may be good at one or more of these skills. Some of us have to learn all this from watching others and reading on.

For many of us, managing our time efficiently and effectively is a skill we have to acquire, and there are many management experts around willing to offer magic formulae for success – not to mention all those specially designed diaries, books, training courses and videos, all offering methods and guidelines for better time management.

There's money in teaching time management. It was the eighteenth-century American statesman Benjamin Franklin who coined the phrase 'Time is money' and people running businesses have never forgotten it. But it's not enough just to *know* that you should be more efficient – or, as a manager, simply to go around shouting at people who are in a muddle or arriving late. You need to look at some commonsense guidelines behind the problems and solve them before they occur.

Self-confidence is the key

There's a saying that 'Procrastination is the thief of time' and procrastination – meaning delaying or postponing actions – is a favourite tactic of people who are scared of the consequences of taking a decision. You may not want to arrive on time at a meeting because you'd really rather not go at all and somehow, by postponing the evil hour when you have to meet an apparent threat, you hope subconsciously to avoid it altogether.

But, as time management experts point out, those lengthy and alarming jobs won't get any easier with delay – and, indeed, may grow worse and turn into even bigger problems.

Train yourself to prioritise

When you're doing any job you need to be able to set priorities. But prioritising is absolutely essential when you're running your own business because without it – especially at the start – you end up running round in circles and in danger of not getting anything done properly.

Here are ten time-wasters to watch out for:

1. non-essential phone calls;
2. chatting with colleagues;
3. filling in forms and other easy routine jobs;
4. non-essential meetings;
5. chasing up people who aren't available;
6. reading junk mail;
7. panics over orders/deliveries etc.;
8. panics over faulty equipment/running out of stationery etc.;
9. interruptions to essential work;
10. trying to do everything yourself.

What are your key tasks for the day?

Learn to prioritise and delegate. Setting your priorities is one of the key factors in increasing your efficiency. When everything seems to need your instant attention, you need to distinguish between tasks that are important and tasks which are urgent. Tasks which are for today and tasks which are for tomorrow. Tasks which only you can do and tasks which someone else can handle. You need to make the best use you can of the time you have, because time is money – you can't spend it twice.

So how do you stop yourself getting bogged down with trivia that could be done by others or even by yourself – but not now, later, at a time when the pressure on your precious time is less?

Most time management systems – and you can pay a lot for a complete system with its own special diary if you want to – advise you to sort out your priorities by making lists. The first aim of the lists – which should be brief and not detailed – is to sort out your timing priorities.

List 1   Today – must do
List 2   Tomorrow – must do
List 3   This week – must do

Start with List 1: divide this list into things which will make money and things which are routine tasks. Then decide which is the most important task and start doing it. Don't sit around admiring your lists – get on with things! If you get stuck on your most important task, start doing the next task on the list and do everything in the order it appears on your list.

If you are not a sole trader, you can put initials against the different tasks and make sure you know who is going to do each task and then allocate them. If you are a sole trader, perhaps there are tasks which you can allocate to others – your book-keeper, your accountant, your wife/husband/partner if they help you out etc. Is it worth you paying someone to do some part-time work for you because you are spending hours on routines tasks which don't earn you money?

At the end of the day, review your lists and transfer the things that still need to be done to List 2 – tomorrow. There should only be a few things left over.

Avoid the 'wish list' trap

The worst technique many people have is to keep putting lots of non-specific tasks with no deadlines on to their lists every day. These make you think you're not coping. Tasks such as 'Buy new computer' or 'Get new secretary'. What is wrong with these ideas? Well, everything really. Each of them is a project in itself, requiring several steps to complete and they cannot be tackled in a few minutes in a busy day. They need detailed planning and they need scheduling into your timetable in a more manageable form – starting with List 3.

You can deal with these shapeless wish list tasks by scheduling yourself 20 minutes or half an hour just to deal with that particular problem and nothing else. Then you should find you move it forward, and it changes shape to the more precise and definite task of 'Go to computer shop' and 'Contact secretarial agency' or 'Draw up advertisement for secretary'.

Is your workplace ordered or chaotic?

Of course, in order to plough on efficiently, your working environment needs to be efficient, so another target for time management specialists is therefore, not surprisingly, the chaotic workplace.

Whatever kind of work you do, you need systems for dealing with routine, everyday tasks, and you and everyone working with you should know what is expected of them, and where to find the files or supplies to work efficiently. There should be no need for permanently untidy piles of papers or odd bits of equipment with no apparent use. The old saying: 'A tidy desk means a tidy mind', which used to be taught to schoolchildren, is worth considering when you look at your own workplace.

But it's not just tidiness and order that's important for efficiency. You can't work well with constant interruptions or if you have to take telephone calls when you're in the middle of a complicated task. People who have too much to do at once often get a glazed expression which means they're not taking in crucially important messages at all. Their real heartfelt wish is that everyone would just go away and leave them alone.

Even when you're a very small business or working on your own, there will be times when you need to be protected from incoming calls and from interruptions to meetings, and should be able to rely on your answerphone or on people working for you, and not have to worry about trivial details.

Can you afford to go on being late?

Lack of confidence is often a crucial factor for people who are not necessarily inefficient at their work, but are frequently late for appointments.

Some people are always late because of their insecurity, which leads to a subconscious horror of arriving early and not knowing what to say. So they would rather be late than early because being late means there's always a start to the conversation, making apologies and going through excuses about the traffic, or public transport, or the pressure of work, followed by getting straight down to business, because there's no time to do anything else.

If that sentence seems rather breathless, well so are the lives of people who can't seem to help being late, but people who are always late need to bring rules of commonsense and self-discipline into their lives. This isn't as easy as it sounds because, as some time management experts point out, most time management techniques work against human nature – which is usually looking for the easiest way out. But, if you are not a naturally well-organised person, you will have to learn to plan ahead.

Planning tips for late people

Ask yourself these questions.

- Do you need to plan a journey the night before you go?
- Should you plan a meeting the night before?
- When should you build in time for forward planning tomorrow during today?
- What time should you start getting ready to travel to a meeting? Have you written down the time to pack up work and start to get ready in your diary? Can you stick to it?
- Should you write down a time to leave in the morning and stick to it?
- Do you really want to be early or on time?
- Would you prefer to be a little bit late?
- Is this really a professional attitude?
- Are you damaging your professional image by being late?

Stop busking

Busking is for the streets. Are you by nature a busker – always trying to get by without preparation? And does it really work? Are you doing your best or do you find yourself thinking after a meeting – if only I'd brought those figures/that map/that report/ those slides/those videos; if only I'd prepared an answer to that tricky question; if only I'd briefed myself before I went to sleep/ while I was travelling to the meeting; if only – if only – I just hope I don't lose that chance of business?

THE IMPORTANCE OF CONTACTS

All things being equal, people will buy from a friend. All things being not quite so equal, people will still buy from a friend.

Mark McCormack, *What They Don't Teach You at Harvard Business School*

If you are a sole trader, you obviously run some risks of professional isolation. You may work entirely on your own, so how are you going to keep up with changes in your business, new trends and so on? Also, how can you keep your morale up and get things in perspective if they aren't going as well as you'd like? These problems of professional isolation can also apply to people in partnerships and in small limited companies.

Professional and trade organisations

You may find that joining a professional or trade organisation directly related to your skills will be useful – though it depends how dynamic the organisation is. At the very least, you should get newsletters with up-to-date information, and you may be able to attend regular meetings where you can meet people in the same field and make some contacts who will help you to keep your ups and downs in proportion when compared with theirs.

You may also find it helpful to join a general club or network of business people. There are chambers of commerce in many towns, plus networks for women and for men. Being a member of a sports club will both keep you fit and plug you into a different environment. If you are a member of a church, synagogue or mosque, you can build a network of local contacts, acquaintances and support – all of which can be vital when you need to take a step back, have some time off and relax away from your usual day-to-day cares.

In other words, many forms of clubs or groups can give you the useful support of people who don't just see you in a business context and broaden your horizons by plugging you into something outside your business. They may also provide you with that vital contact when you're stuck and need some advice about a tricky business problem.

If someone asks me for a product I've never supplied before, I just ring up the Birmingham Chamber of Commerce and they put me in touch with some useful contacts or they fax me information from handbooks with lists of possible contacts. Before I became a member, I used to spend hours in the library looking for information and I wasted a lot of time.

Ted Bonner, E.G. Exports

How big will you get?

Being a member of an organisation, whether it's a parent-teacher committee or a golf club, means plugging into a network, and networks of all kinds can help you to cope with the stresses, strains and responsibilities of running your own show.

How big that show should be is a decision you will have to take. Some people just do not want to grow beyond a small business run by themselves or with a business partner. Others will have ambitions to expand from Day 1 and would never be happy remaining small.

9

Growing your Business

■

There are no short cuts. In my opinion, anyone who makes it very rich very quick – within a few years – has done it either because they've had a large amount of capital or because they've broken the rules. It takes time to build up a business. In normal circumstances it takes about three years for a business to become established. Given the recession, I would say it's more like five years.

Fiona Price, Fiona Price and Partners Limited

SYSTEMS FOR A GROWING BUSINESS

WHETHER YOU start up your business as a sole trader, a partnership or as a limited company, you are very unlikely to start off in your first year with a turnover of a million or more. But, even as a sole trader or a partnership of just two people, you may find that your business grows sufficiently for you to consider changing it to a limited company. This means a change in legal status for your business and in tax status for you.

All directors have to be employed by their companies and pay tax on PAYE. They cannot be self-employed as defined by the Inland Revenue. However, although this may appear to be a disadvantage, there are advantages such as the limitation of your liability for company debts and the fact that it may be easier to raise money as a limited company.

If you are a sole trader, you double your staff by taking on just one person full-time and it can seem like a very big step when you take on your very first employee, whether full-time or part-time. But if you are successful in generating business, you may soon have to consider taking on more full-time or part-time staff. You may have to subcontract some of your work to others or use consultants to help you move into a business area new to you. How can you avoid losing control of your business? How can you keep the tight control of your own business you had when you started?

In this chapter, we'll be looking at some useful systems for helping your business to keep going and keep growing. If you *do* grow your business, you also have to decide whether you want it to remain small – a micro-business or a lifestyle business, intended only to support you and your lifestyle. Or whether you want to go for real growth and become a bigger business.

Teamwork or solo flyer?

Research into businesses started in recent years by one person alone, both in Britain and in the US, has shown that a one-person micro-business will often stay micro-sized, not only because the person running it wants to stay small, but also because entrepreneurs working largely on their own will never develop the business skills needed to go for growth into a medium or even a large organisation. They will never stand back and see where they might take their skills if they thought a bit bigger. They may not want to think bigger at all.

There is evidence that businesses started by teams, or businesses where sole traders join up to work together and form a partnership or company, have far more chance of growing beyond the micro-business level. The old saying that 'two heads are better than one' seems to work well in business, where teamwork can produce results which are far more than a mere multiplication of the number of people involved.

The vision thing

Another intangible element in the success of a business is how you and others see it. Do you want to be the best in your field – or do you just want to survive?

Do you have a vision of your future and how you intend to get there? How do others see you and your business? Do they see you as the best – or at least one of the best – or have you managed in a short time to become merely ordinary? Your vision of your business can not only help you grow, it can help you to sustain your market share and hold on in difficult times.

Mission statements

In the 1970s and 1980s, the idea of a mission statement for companies became very fashionable. Some were printed on headed paper and in annual reports, and while in some cases they may have had relevance, in others they frequently appeared embarrassing and irrelevant; something extra and ill-fitting, grafted on to a firm's public presentation because of a fad in management theory.

I can never see the words 'Our Mission Statement' without hearing the music of *Star Trek* and the lugubrious announcement at the start, complete with the split infinitive 'These are the voyages of the Starship Enterprise. Its mission: to boldly go where no man has gone before.' Now that's what I call a mission statement. After that, everything else is an anti-climax. Lacking, you might say, in cosmic reach.

Mission statements – some people swear by them, some swear at them. A mission statement can have its uses, but you don't have to publish externally what you think you're about. You can devise your own mission statement and keep it as an internal weapon. For instance, 'To be the best management consultancy in the Midlands'; 'Always to provide excellent service to all my customers'; 'To build a business which will offer good quality children's clothes at prices ordinary people can afford'.

The most important characteristics of a successful mission statement are that the statement expresses the overriding business goals of the company clearly, memorably and realistically, and that it fits in with how all the staff see the company. If it is widely known throughout your business and is useful to your organisation, you may find it useful in building team spirit. If it is short and snappy and non-pompous, you may feel it is useful to put in your promotional literature.

OMBs

OMB stands for owner managed business and is a term used to describe businesses which can be small or which can have turnovers of millions of pounds a year. The common thread linking them all is that they are all companies managed by their owners, often the people who founded them.

Leading accountancy firm Touche Ross, which does frequent surveys of owner-managed businesses, says OMBs have many advantages in terms of tight centres of power and decision-making, but some of their main faults are:

- *lack of adequate management systems* – leading to a freewheeling approach to business planning, probably as heavily influenced by the individual culture, style and abilities of the owner manager as they are by business needs;
- *lack of long-term forward planning* – this means short-term changes can cause business plans to disintegrate;
- *not enough use of formal plans put into writing* – this can lead to inconsistencies among directors with plans changing on almost a daily basis, depending on whims, moods and short-term circumstances.

Touche Ross advises that long-term business objectives should be set for all OMBs. These should set out the broad direction of the business, goals and major actions on a three to five-year basis. This long-term plan then sets the framework for a detailed short-term plan for the coming year. These conclusions can apply whether the company has a turnover of £100,000 a year, £1 million, £5 million or even £50 million.

So, do you have a vision of expansion or do you want to stay more or less where you are? It's your decision – either alone, if you're a sole trader, or with your partners or co-directors.

But even if you're a sole trader you may have a husband/wife/

partner who has an interest in you and your income. You may assume you know what they think and want, but have you really discussed it with them? People can have strong feelings either way – 'But I always thought you wanted to have a bigger business' or 'But I always thought you didn't want to employ people and you wanted to work on your own'.

But I always thought . . . These words can reveal fundamental differences and can lead to splits, either personal or professional. If you have business partners or co-directors, are you all rowing in the same race? In the same boat? On the same river?

> *We determined our objectives 21 years ago, and the insistence on pursuing these objectives is the key to our success. The transition of small business to large can be done, but you have to want to do it. It comes down to a matter of determination and hard work. Getting up before the others. Staying up later than the others.*

> Lord Hanson, quoted in *Small Businesses – How to Succeed and Survive* by Brian Jenks

Recession busters

Whatever your current size of operation, how are you coping in the current uncertain business environment? All businesses need to develop strategies to ride out downturns and recessions.

In 1993, London-based OC & C Strategy Consultants surveyed 250 of Britain's leading companies to find out which had been profitable over the previous 5 years and managed to maintain profit growth. Despite $\frac{2}{3}$ of the top 25 companies being in recession-proof sectors, such as food retailing and wholesaling, telecommunications and pharmaceuticals, the survey found their success was mainly due to adopting at least one of the following three strategies:

- aggressively pursuing and executing acquisitions;
- quickly capitalising on the troubles of their competitors;
- dominating their sectors.

Chris Outram, a partner in OC & C, said the survey 'shows that it is possible for companies to outrun a low growth economy. Low growth and even recession are not necessarily excuses for reduced profits.'

Further advice

Of course, there are other styles, as David Ogilvy, the legendary advertising guru and founder of agency Ogilvy and Mather, explains: 'First make yourself a reputation for being a creative genius. Second, surround yourself with partners who are better than you are. Third, leave them to get on with it,' he said in an article in the *Sunday Times* on 23 April 1978, on how to succeed in advertising.

This technique seemed to work for him. I'm sure it must apply to other professions and businesses, but, personally, I think that, like walking on water, it's probably harder than it looks.

Conclusion

————•————

EVERYONE'S BUSINESS is different. Even franchisees running the same franchise, with the same standardised business framework, but in different areas and with their own individual personalities, will find differences in their customers and in their own ways of dealing with them. People do vary – a lot.

In this book I've tried to show you a very wide range of different businesses, run by a wide variety of people – each facing different sets of problems in different fields.

But even with the varied selection of businesses covered in this book, there are common themes. Certain comments are repeated and emerge as useful advice for all types of business enterprise. Here are the ten most common tips that emerged from the people interviewed.

1. Get some business training if you can.
2. Make marketing a priority.
3. Use free editorial and develop your public relations.
4. Join clubs or networks.
5. Keep fit.
6. Keep track of your money.
7. Be prepared to be a jack, or jill, of all trades.
8. Be prepared to work long hours.
9. Learn to trust your instincts.
10. Believe in yourself.

These guidelines are helpful because they make it clear that anyone can run their own show – but they must know a little of what they're letting themselves in for. Hopefully, this book can help.

Good luck!

CHECKLIST ONE

Income tax, National Insurance and VAT

Telephone numbers accurate as of 1 April 1995

Income tax

Inland Revenue
Somerset House
London WC2R 1LB
0171-438 6420 Public enquiries

Information about tax, self-employment etc.

National Insurance

Contributions Agency
Department of Social Security
Longbenton
Newcastle upon Tyne NE98 1YX
Tel: 016451 56563 Calls charged at local rate

Social Security Advice Line for Employers and the Self-Employed on 0800 393539 Freephone (no charge). Or contact your local Social Security Office listed in your local phone book under *Social Security, Department of*

VAT (Value Added Tax)

Customs and Excise

For information on VAT registration, deregistration or reregistration:

- if you are in the London area ring 0345 112114;
- England outside London, ring your local VAT office, listed in the telephone book or *Yellow Pages* under Customs and Excise;
- Scotland, Wales and Northern Ireland, ring your local VAT office, listed in the telephone book or *Yellow Pages* under Customs and Excise;
- Ireland, ring Dublin (010-353) 18746821 or write to:
  Central Registry Office
  9–15 Upper O'Connell Street
  Dublin 1
  Ireland

Self-Assessment and the tax system

The principle behind the change to Self-Assessment of tax is that each taxpayer has to work out their own liability for tax without the Inland Revenue having to make an assessment or calculate the tax due. It's a move towards the American style system of making the public do the work the Government tax collectors used to do.

There are legal requirements for maintaining and keeping records and a different style of tax return with automatic penalties if returns are not submitted on time. This change to a new system means the Inland Revenue will become more of an 'auditor' who checks on people's figures, and less of a tax collector who decides exactly what you pay and then demands you pay it.

Self assessment means that self-employed people will be charged to tax on profits shown in their accounts drawn up to a date in a current tax year instead of the old system of being taxed on the preceding year. All new businesses starting as sole traders or partnerships on or after 6 April 1994 are taxed on the current year basis. Existing businesses will start the new system in April 1997, i.e. the tax year 1997–8. Check with your local Inland Revenue office for details and information on how this affects you.

CHECKLIST TWO

Copyright

Telephone numbers accurate as of 1 April 1995

British Copyright Council
Copyright House
29–33 Berners Street
London W1P 4AA
Fax no: 0171-359 1895
Postal or fax enquiries only

Department of Trade and Industry
Intellectual Property Policy
    Directorate
Copyright Enquiries
Room 4/5, Hazlitt House
45 Southampton Buildings
London WC2A 1AR
Tel: 0171-438 4778

Institute of Practitioners in
    Advertising
44 Belgrave Square
London SW1X 8QS
Tel: 0171-235 7020

National Union of Journalists
314 Gray's Inn Road
London WC1X 8DP
Tel: 0171-278 7916

The Patent Office
Patents Enquiry Desk
25 Southampton Buildings
London WC2A 1AY
Tel: 0171-438 4778

Patents Enquiry Desk
The Patent Office
Cardiff Road
Newport
Gwent NP9 1RH
Tel: 01633 815162

Trade Marks and Service Marks
    Enquiry Desk
The Patent Office
(address as above)
Tel: 01633 814706/9

Performing Rights Society Limited
29 Berners Street
London W1P 4AA
Tel: 0171-580 5544

Writers Guild
430 Edgware Road
London W2 1EH
Tel: 0171-723 8074

CHECKLIST THREE

Importing and exporting

Telephone numbers accurate as of 1 April 1995

EXPORTING

British Exporters Association
16 Dartmouth Street
London SW1H 9BL
Tel: 0171-222 5419

British Overseas Trade Board
Export Market Information
    Centre
1–19 Victoria Street
London SW1H 0ET
Tel: 0171-215 5444/5
Fairs and Promotions Branch
Tel: 0171-276 2414
plus several regional offices

*Croner's Reference Book for
    Exporters*
Croner Publications
Croner House
London Road
Kingston upon Thames
Surrey KT2 6SR
Tel: 0181-547 3333

Export Credit Guarantee
Department

Crown Building
Cathays Park
Cardiff CF1 3NH
Tel: 01222 824100
This is the head office – there are
several regional offices

The Institute of Export
Export House
64 Clifton Street
London EC2A 4HB
Tel: 0171-247 9812

General advice on exporting is also
available from chambers of
commerce, Training and Enterprise
Councils, the Confederation of
British Industry, and professional
organisations dealing with
management, marketing and
insurance.

IMPORTING

British Importers' Confederation
Rooms 309–315, 3rd Floor
Kemp House

152–160 City Road
London EC1V 2NP
Tel: 0171-490 7262

*Croner's Reference Book for
   Importers*
Croner Publications
Croner House
London Road
Kingston upon Thames
Surrey KT2 6SR
Tel: 0181-547 3333

Department of Trade and Industry
Import Licensing Branch
Queensway House
West Precinct
Billingham
Cleveland TS23 2NF
Tel: 01642 364333/4

General advice on importing is also
available from chambers of
commerce, Training and Enterprise
Councils, the Confederation of
British Industry, and professional
organisations dealing with
management, marketing and
insurance.

CHECKLIST FOUR

Useful organisations

Telephone numbers accurate as of 1 April 1995

ACAS
(The Advisory Conciliation and
Arbitration Service)
11/12 St James's Square
London SW1Y 4LA
Tel: 0171-214 6000

Agencies – see FRES

Department of Employment

London and SE England
Employment Agencies Licensing
   Office
Exchange House
60 Exchange Road
Watford
Herts WD1 7HH
Tel: 01923 210706

Midlands, SW England and Wales
Employment Agencies Licensing
   Office
Room 1410, Cumberland House
200 Broad Street
Birmingham B15 1PQ
Tel: 0121-608 9744

North of England and Scotland
Employment Agencies Licensing
   Office

City House
Leeds LS1 4YU
Tel: 01132 836539

Arts Council of Great Britain
14 Great Peter Street
London SW1P 3NQ
Tel: 0171-338 0111

**Association of British Chambers of
   Commerce**
9 Tufton Street
London SW1P 3QB
Tel: 0171-222 1555

British Franchise Association
Franchise Chambers
Thames View
Newtown Road
Henley-on-Thames
Oxon RG9 1HG
Tel: 01491 578049

BSI
(British Standards Institution)
Linford Wood
Milton Keynes
MK14 6LE
Tel: 01908 220022

Business in the Community
8 Stratton Street
London W1X 5FD
Tel: 0171-629 1600

Business Names – see Companies Registration

Business Networks – see Association of British Chambers of Commerce, Institute of Directors, Rotary International of Britain and Ireland, TUC and Women's Business Networks

Career Development Loans
Co-operative Bank plc
PO Box 101
1 Balloon Street
Manchester M60 4EP

Barclays Bank local branches

Clydesdale Bank local branches

Companies Registration Office – England and Wales
Companies House
Crown Way
Cardiff CF4 3UZ
Tel: 01222 388588

Companies Registration Office – Scotland
102 George Street
Edinburgh EH2 3DJ
Tel: 0131-225 5774

Companies Registry – Ireland
IDB House
64 Chichester Street
Belfast BT1 4JX
Tel: 01232 234488

Contributions Agency – see Checklist 1

Co-operatives

For English Regional Offices contact:
ICOM (Industrial and Common Ownership Movement)
Vassalli House
20 Central Road
Leeds LS1 6DE
Tel: 01132 461738/37

Northern Ireland Co-operative Development Agency
23–25 Shipquay Street
Londonderry
N. Ireland BT48 6DL
Tel: 01504 371733

Scottish Co-operative Development Agency
Templeton Business Centre
Templeton Street
Bridgeton
Glasgow G40 1DA
Tel: 0141-554 3797

Wales Co-operative Centre
Llandaff Court
Fairwater Road
Llandaff
Cardiff CF5 2XP
Tel: 01222 554955

CRE
(Commission for Racial Equality)
Elliot House
10–12 Allington Street
London SW1E 5EH
Tel: 0171-828 7022

CRE – Regional Offices

Birmingham Tel: 0121-632 4544
Manchester Tel: 0161-831 7782
Leeds Tel: 01132 434413
Leicester Tel: 01162 517852
Edinburgh Tel: 0131 226 5186

Croner's Reference Book for the
Self-employed and Smaller
Business
Croner House
London Road
Kingston upon Thames
Surrey KT2 6SR
Tel: 0181-547 3333
Updated monthly

Customs and Excise – see Checklist 1

Data Protection Registrar

Wycliffe House
Water Lane
Wilmslow
Cheshire SK9 5AF
Tel: 01625 535777/01625 535711

Designs – see Checklist 2

Disabled – contact your local JobCentre and ask to see the disability employment adviser or your local TEC (Training and Enterprise Council) for advice on training and retraining.

Disabled Organisations

RADAR (Royal Society for
Disability and Rehabilitation)
Tel: 0171-637 5400

DTI

(Department of Trade and
Industry)
1–19 Victoria Street
London SW1H 0ET
Tel: 0171-215 7877 (information
line)

European Community

England
Commission of the European
Community
Jean Monnet House
8 St Storey's Gate
London SW1P 3AT
Tel: 0171-973 1947 (information
line)

Northern Ireland
Commission of the European
Community
Windsor House
9–15 Bedford Street
Belfast BT2 7EG
Tel: 01232 240708

Scotland
Commission of the European
Community
9 Alva Street
Edinburgh EH2 2PH
Tel: 0131-225 2058

Wales
Commission of the European
Community
4 Cathedral Road
Cardiff CF1 9SG
Tel: 01222 371631

European Parliament Information Office
2 Queen Anne's Gate
London SW1H 9AA
Tel: 0171-222 0411

Employment

England and Wales
Department of Employment
Caxton House
Tothill Street
London SW1H 9NF
Tel: 0171-273 6969 (public
    inquiries)

Northern Ireland
Employment in Northern Ireland
Local Enterprise Development
    Unit
The Small Business Agency
Tel: 01232 491031

Scotland
Employment Services
Employment Intelligence Service
    Enquiries
Argyle House
3 Lady Lawson Street
Edinburgh EH3 9ST
Tel: 0131-221 4151

Employment agencies – see FRES

Equal Opportunities Commission
Overseas House
Quay Street
Manchester M3 3HN
Tel: 0161-833 9244
Offers advice on equal pay,
maternity pay, sex discrimination,
sexual harassment and may provide
help with legal costs.

Family Business – see Stoy Centre for Family Business

Federation of Small Businesses
32 St Anne's Road West
Lytham St Anne's
Lancashire FY8 1NY
Tel: 01253 720911

Franchising – see British Franchise Association

Freelance Media Group
c/o The Groucho Club
44 Dean Street
London W1V 5AP
Tel: 0171-439 4605

FRES
(Federation of Recruitment and
    Employment Services)
36 Mortimer Street
London W1N 7RB
Tel: 0171-323 4300

Greater London Business Centre
Tel: 0800 222999 (Freephone)

Health and Safety Executive
St Hugh's House
Stanley Precinct
Bootle
Merseyside
Tel: 0151-951 4000

Home Run
79 Black Lion Lane
London W6 9BG
Tel/Fax: 0181-846 9244

Income Tax – see Checklist 1

Institute of Directors
116 Pall Mall
London SW1Y 5ED
Tel: 0171-839 1233

JobCentres
For your local JobCentre look in
the phone book under
Employment Service

**Jobsharing – see New Ways to
Work**

**National Association of
  Shopkeepers**
Lynch House
91 Mansfield Rd
Nottingham NG1 3FN
Tel: 01159 475046

**National Insurance – see
  Checklist 1**

New Ways to Work
309 Upper Street
London N1 2TY
Tel: 0171-226 4026

Patents – see Checklist 2

Prince's Youth Business Trust
5 Cleveland Place
London SW1Y 6JJ
Tel: 0171-321 6500
*Offers start-up help to people aged
18 to 29*

**Prince's Scottish Youth Business
  Trust**
Mercantile Chambers
6th Floor, 53 Bothwell Street
Glasgow G2 6TS
Tel: 0141-248 4999

**RSI Association (Repetitive Strain
  Injury Association)**
Chapel House
152 High Street
Yiewsley
West Drayton
Middx UV7 7BD
Tel: 01895 431134

**Rotary International of Britain and
  Ireland**
Kinwarton Road
Alcester
Warwickshire B49 6BP
Tel: 01789 765411

Royal Town Planning Institute
26 Portland Place
London W1N 4BE
Tel: 0171-636 9107

Rural Development Commission
141 Castle Street
Salisbury SP1 3TP
Tel: 01722 336255

**Shops – see National Association of
Shopkeepers**

**Small Firms Business Information
  Service**
London and SE England – see
Greater London Business Centre.
Rest of England, Scotland, N.
Ireland and Wales – see TECs

Sports Council
16 Upper Woburn Place
London WC1H 0QP
Tel: 0171-388 1277

Sports Council for Northern Ireland
House of Sport
Upper Malone Street
Belfast BT9 5LA
Tel: 01232 381222

**Scottish Enterprise (formerly
    Scottish Development Agency)**
120 Bothwell Street
Glasgow G2 7JP
Tel: 0141-248 2700

Stoy Centre for Family Business
8 Baker Street
London W1M 1DA
Tel: 0171-486 5888

**TECs (Training and Enterprise
    Councils)**
Your local JobCentre can put you
in touch with your local TEC – see
JobCentres or ring the Department
of Employment, Sheffield
Tel: 01142 753275

Trademarks – see Checklist 2

TUC (Trades Union Congress)
23–28 Great Russell Street
London WC1B 3LS
Tel: 0171-636 4030

VAT – see Checklist 1

Welsh Development Agency
Pearl House
Greyfriars Road
Cardiff CF1 3XX
Tel: 01222 223666

CHECKLIST FIVE

Business names and addresses

CHAPTER ONE

Peter Juniper
Piano Tuning and Repair Service
Telephone enquiries only
Tel: 0181-421 8307
or: 01288 84 320

Ted Bonner
E.G. Exports
Bron-y-Bryn
New Road
Caunsall
Kidderminster DY11 5YN
Tel: 01562 850777

CHAPTER TWO

Tony King
TWK Alarms
123 Raithby Drive
Hawkley Hall
Wigan WN3 5PZ
Tel: 01942 39295

Rex Harden
Forget-Me-Not
56 Pirton Lane

Churchdown
Gloucester GL3 2SJ
Tel: 01452 712042

Pauline Davies
Aunties (Great Britain) Limited
56 Coleshill Terrace
Llanelli
Dyfed SA15 3DA
Tel: 01554 770077

Ann Corsie
Reading School of Aromatherapy
   and Healing
The Penthouse
2 Glebe Road
Reading RG2 7AG
Tel: 01734 871865

CHAPTER FOUR

Mark Prest
Mark Prest Glass
Studio 23
Manchester Craft Centre
17 Oak Street
Manchester M4 5JB
Tel: 0161-839 8713

CHAPTER FIVE

Colin Murphy
The Bookkeeping Bureau
Barley Mow Centre
10 Barley Mow Passage
London W4 4PH
Tel: 0181-994 6477

Celia Kemsley
Market Openings/Peak
   Performance
59c Goodge Street
London W1P 1FA
Tel: 0171-637 3174

CHAPTER SEVEN

Barbara Kidd
Herforder UK Ltd
Withinlee
Withinlee Road
Prestbury
Cheshire SK10 4AT
Tel: 01625 828334

CHAPTER EIGHT

Mary Spillane
CMB Image Consultants
66 Abbey Business Centre
Ingate Place
London SW8 3NS
Tel: 0171-627 5211

CHAPTER NINE

Fiona Price
Fiona Price and Partners Limited
33 Great Queen Street
Covent Garden
London WC2B 5AA
Tel: 0171-430 0366

ADDITIONAL HELP FROM

Jacquie Hyde
Field Flowers
Eardisley
Herefordshire HR3 6NA
Tel: 01544 327750

Deanna Maclaren
c/o Sheild Land Associates
Tel: 0171-405 9351

Angela Maclean
Rainbow Cleaning Services
H27 The Avenue
11th Avenue North
Team Valley
Tyne and Wear
NE11 0NJ
Tel: 0191-491 4080

Anna Murphy
AA Music
40 Nettlehill Road
Lisburn
Co. Antrim
Northern Ireland
BT28 3HA
Tel: 01846 607155

Mark Wray
Willy Wiper
9/13 Pleasant Hill Street
Liverpool L8 5SA
Tel: 0151-709 2271

Booklist

SELF-EMPLOYMENT AND SMALL BUSINESS

A Business Plan by Alan West (Natwest Small Business Bookshelf, Pitman)

Croner's Reference Book For The Self-Employed And Smaller Business (Croner Publications Limited)

Going Freelance by Godfrey Golzen (Granada)

Home Is Where The Office Is – A Practical Handbook For Teleworking From Home by Andrew Bibby (Headway/Hodder & Stoughton)

How To Run A Part-Time Business by Barrie Hawkins (Piatkus Books)

Importing For The Small Business by Mag Morris (Kogan Page)

Making Money From Your Home – Over 100 Ways To Earn Extra Income by Hazel Evans (Piatkus)

Making Profits – A Six Month Action Plan For The Small Business by Malcolm Bird (Piatkus Books)

101 Ways to Succeed As An Independent Consultant by Timothy R. V. Foster (Kogan Page)

Small Businesses – How To Succeed And Survive by Brian Jenks (Headway/Hodder and Stoughton)

Starting A Business On A Shoestring by Michel Syrett and Chris Dunn (Penguin)

Working From Home – 201 Ways To Make Money by Marianne Gray (Piatkus)

BUSINESS SKILLS

Achieving Results Through Time Management by Philip Atkinson (Pitman Books)

Better Business Writing – How To Give Extra Power And Clarity To Your Memos, Letters And Reports by Maryann V. Piotrowski (Piatkus Books)

The Complete Book Of Business Etiquette by Lynne Brennan and David Block (Piatkus Books)

The Complete Time Management System by Christian Godefroy and John Clark (Piatkus Books)

Confident Conversation – How To Talk In Any Business Or Social Situation by Dr Lillian Glass (Piatkus Books)

Getting Past No – Negotiating With Difficult People by William Ury (Business Books)

Getting To Yes – Negotiating An Agreement Without Giving In by Roger Fisher and William Ury (Business Books – second Edition)

How To Collect The Money You Are Owed by Malcolm Bird (Piatkus Books)

How To Master Finance by Terry Gasking (Business Books)

Time Management by Martin Scott (Century Business)

The 24 Hour Business Plan by Ron Johnson (Century Business)

MARKETING AND PROMOTION

Be Your Own PR Expert by Bill Penn (Piatkus Books)

Creating Customers – An Action Plan For Maximising Sales, Publicity and Promotion by David H Bangs (Piatkus)

How to Close Every Sale by Joe Girard with Robert L. Shook (Piatkus Books)

How to Make Your Fortune Through Network Marketing by John Bremner (Piatkus Books)

How to Succeed in Network Marketing by Leonard Hawkins (Piatkus Books)

The Popcorn Report – Revolutionary Trend Predictions For Marketing In The 90s by Faith Popcorn (Century Business)

Telephone Selling Techniques That Really Work by Bill Good (Piatkus Books)

WOMEN

Enterprising Women – The Lives Of Successful Business Women by Carol Dix (Bantam)

The Influential Woman – How To Achieve Success Without Losing Your Femininity by Lee Bryce (Piatkus Books)

Travelling Alone – A Guide For Working Women by Roberta Bailey (Macdonald Optima)

GENERAL

The Age of Unreason by Charles Handy (Business Books)

Buying A Shop by E. A. Jensen (self-published)

Career Turnaround – How To Apply Corporate Strategy Techniques To Your Own Career by John Viney and Stephanie Jones (Thorsons)

Creating Abundance – How To Bring Wealth And Fulfilment Into Your Life by Andrew Ferguson (Piatkus Books)

Going For It! How To Succeed As An Entrepreneur by Victor Kiam (Collins)

How To Be Headhunted by Yvonne Sarch (Business Books)

It Ain't As Easy As It Looks: Ted Turner's Amazing Story by Porter Bibb (Virgin Books)

Living With Stress by Cary L. Cooper, Rachel D. Cooper and Lynn H. Eaker (Penguin)

Streetwise Franchising by Danielle Baillieu (Hutchinson)

What Color Is Your Parachute? by Richard Nelson Bolles (Ten Speed Press)

What They Don't Teach You At Harvard Business School by Mark McCormack (Collins)

Which Way Now? – How To Plan And Develop A Successful Career by Bridget Wright (Piatkus Books)

Index